I, Yeshua
Awakener.

Lars Gimstedt   ©PsychosynthesisForum.com 2014

© **PsykosyntesForum, 2014**

No part of this book may be reproduced in any form, except for the quotation of brief passages in criticism or reviews, without the expressed permission of the publisher: mail@psykosyntesforum.se.

Revision date July 26 2014.

ISBN
978-91-981941-0-4   (EPUB version)
978-91-981941-1-1   (LIT   version)
978-91-981941-2-8   (MOBI version)
978-91-981941-3-5   (PDF   version)
978-91-981941-4-2   (Paper back)

The MOBI (Kindle) version is available on Amazon.com and other Amazon internet stores. The other versions, including the Swedish versions, are available at http://psykosyntesforum.se/Yeshua.htm

Typeface Bookman Old 12. Page size 6x9" (15,24 x 22,86 cm). Margins: hor 2,0 / vert 2,5.

Lars Gimstedt   ©*PsychosynthesisForum.com 2014*

About the author:

Lars Gimstedt works as a psychotherapist in Linkoping, Sweden. His formal training was as a quantum physicist, and he has worked as an engineer and a manager in corporate business for 30 years.

In the middle of his life, he started to study Psychosynthesis, CBT and NLP, and worked part time as a psychotherapist during ten years, until he started to work full time in his company PsychosynthesisForum.com in 2003 with life and leadership coaching, psychotherapy and with internet e-courses and e-books.

Previous books by Lars Gimstedt:

Stairway: 10 Steps to Heaven. (March 2014)

About this book:

Who is Jesus? Is he the one described by Paulus and the evangelists in the Bible? Or can a clearer picture of the real person Jesus emerge if one limits oneself to read only what historical data points at being plausible direct quotes?

If Jesus, or Yeshua as his name was in his native tongue Aramaic, would have written his gospel himself, how would that book be?

This book is a proposal for how His own gospel *could* have been. It is based on what modern history has revealed about the time of His life, and is also based on the parts of religious scripture that seem to be possible to confirm historically.

Because historical data, despite new findings, are still extremely scarce, the book is naturally mostly pure fiction, and it is up to you, the reader of this book, to assess what you are willing to accept and what you feel you must reject.

In either case, this book can hopefully inspire you to search for more information about the true Yeshua bar Yosef from Nazareth, the poor wood-worker from an obscure little village in a remote part of the Roman Empire that with his words and deeds has influenced mankind for two millennia.

"Lars Gimstedt has published an interesting book about Jesus, or Yeshua. The book is written as a self-biography by Yeshua, and covers his lifespan from childhood till the very last meeting with his disciples after the resurrection.

The author has done an impressive background study regarding Aramaic and Hebrew names, which are used throughout in the book. It made it easier for me to read the book as an independent story, and not directly synchronize it with the Bible all the time.

It is a book easy to read, the chapters are relatively short, coherent and to the point. Students of A Course in Miracles will detect many references, and especially the main focus, that we are all one with our Creator.

It is refreshing to read a more everyday description of the human life of Yeshua. That his life was not very different from our own in many aspects, so easy to forget. That we are all on the same 'voyage', the return trip to Heaven and the Oneness. He just 'finished' ahead of us.

In the author's foreword in the beginning it is made clear that the story is a fictitious one, but based on some of the available material in the Bible and also A Course in Miracles. Nevertheless it stimulates my own perception and understanding of the human Jesus, which in many ways have been regarded as so special that we 'ordinary' humans could never reach a spiritual advanced state such as he did.

I can recommend the book as worthwhile reading for anyone who is working with, or interested in the spiritual side of life. With its many novel interpretations it can lead to a better understanding of what this is about, for those who dare to think 'outside the box'.

Stjarnsund, Sweden, July 1 2014
Albert Harloff"

(ACIM translator to Norwegian, author of Thy Will Be Done, chairman Swedish ACIM Network.)

Contents

Foreword 9

Chapter 1. December 25 Year 758 AUC.
     The Dream 14

Chapter 2. Maius 17 763.
     The Angel 18

Chapter 3. September 19 764.
     The Rabbi 22

Chapter 4. Aprilis 15 766.
     The Temple 27

Chapter 5. October 1 767.
     Ohannes the Nazarite 38

Chapter 6. Martius 23 769.
     The Essene 47

Chapter 7. Sextilis 14 774.
     The Shudra 54

Chapter 8. Ianuarius 1 780.
     Full vision 61

Chapter 9. December 27 783.
     The Baptist 69

Chapter 10. Ianuarius 13 784.
     The Desert 75

Chapter 11. Februarius 28 784.
     The Mission commences 87

Chapter 12. Aprilis 14 784.
     Miryam Magdalene 94

Chapter 13. December 30 784.
  Rejection. 103
Chapter 14. Quintilis 14 785.
  The Sermon on the Mount. 110
Chapter 15. Sextilis 5 785.
  The Emissaries. 128
Chapter 16. Ianuarius 15 786.
  Ohannes death. 134
Chapter 17. Aprilis 18 786.
  Walking on water. 138
Chapter 18. Quintilis 20 786.
  Preparation. 144
Chapter 19. Quintilus 21 786.
  Transfiguration. 148
Chapter 20. Ianuarius 10 787.
  El'azar. 154
Chapter 21. Aprilis 12 787.
  The Last Supper. 159
Chapter 22. Aprilis 13 787.
  The crucifixion 169
Chapter 23. Aprilis 16 787.
  Resurrection. 179
Chapter 24. Aprilis 19 787.
  The New Beginning 182

Foreword

Jesus came into my life when I was just turning forty. I had been a non-reflecting atheist up to then, but His message as reflected in the book A Course in Miracles made me turn onto a new path, a path towards spiritual awakening.

My interpretation of His message to all his brothers and sisters is:

> You are of God, pure spirit, free of sin and perfect.
>
> But you believe that you have separated yourself from God, to create your own world. Deep down you believe that you have offended God by doing this, that you are sinful and that you deserve punishment. You believe that you can avoid punishment only by repentance and sacrifice.
>
> Many of you have fled from these thoughts by repressing them completely from your conscious mind.
>
> Forgive yourself and forgive your brothers and sisters for these mistaken beliefs. True forgiveness will allow you all to wake up again, to remember who you really are, Gods Children, one with Him, one with me, and one with each other.

> Remembering will make you understand that repentance and sacrifice are not asked of you. Remembering will give you complete peace of mind, because remembering that you are Love will make you extend nothing but Love.

This is a message He has given always. It has always been the same, although given with different words, in different languages, using different symbols, depending on who has been listening, depending on culture, on time period in the history.

His message has been understood by many, who then have remembered who they really are. But it has also become misunderstood and interpreted into forms that have strengthened the mistaken beliefs. This has caused much unnecessary suffering, but is still only a waste of time, as the eventual awakening of everyone to their divine origin is inevitable.

For me personally His message, that came to me twenty-eight years ago, led me into changing my profession from being a physicist and an engineer into becoming a psychotherapist, and after thirty years as technical specialist and manager in cooperate business I have now worked part time as a therapist for ten years and full time another twelve years.

I have tried to apply His message both in my life and in my work as a psychotherapist and as a life coach, both as my value base and also more openly, in e-courses and e-books about spirituality.
(http://PsychosynthesisForum.com)

In the book you now have in your hand, I have been inspired to write a fiction story about His life. I became inspired both by the story *about* and by the message *from* the person Jesus, or Yeshua as his name is in Aramaic, the language He spoke. The story "He" is about to tell in this book reflects *my* personal beliefs on how His life may have been, and *my* personal belief about who Yeshua really was, in contrast to the "official" descriptions in the Bible and in other scriptures.

I hope that you will read this story with an open mind, and that you forgive me for any errors in historic facts that I surely have made due to my lack of expertise. Much of the story will appear to completely contradict narratives about the life of Jesus in the Bible and other books. But, most of these discrepancies come out of my belief that many of these narratives and descriptions of Jesus are based more on religious needs for proving His divinity by making the stories confirm old prophesies, rather than honest attempts to describe actual facts.

Historical data from the time of Jesus are extremely scarce, and available documentation is largely the result of individual authors' and historians' speculations. Below are some of the sources I have used. Even these raise numerous contradictions, and I have made what I think is a reasonable attempt to filter out the data I have found plausible.

www.ccel.org/bible/phillips/CN160-TRAVELS.htm
www.generationword.com/bible_school_notes/13.html to 18.html.

Reza Aslan 2013, Zealot:
The Life and Times of Yeshua of Nazareth.

Jonas Gardell 2009: About Jesus.

The dates are written as used at the time, from the Roman Calendar, Anno Urbis Conditae (**AUC**), which started with the founding of the city of Rome, 753 BC. The names of the months were Martius, Aprilis, Maius, Iunius, Quintilis, Sextilis, September, Oktober, November, December (="the tenth"). Later, 40 AUC, Ianuarius, Februarius were added.

Names are as used at the time, in Aramaic, Latin or ancient Hebrew, instead of the Anglicized names commonly used in English Bible translations.
In alphabetical order:

Elisabeth	Elisheba	("Yahweh is abundance")
James	Hakob	("May Yahweh protect")
Jesus	Yeshua	("Yahweh is salvation")
John	Ohannes	("Yahweh is gracious")
Joseph	Yosef	("He will add")
Judas	Yehudah	("Praised")
Mary	Miryam	("Beloved")
Peter	Petros	("Rock")
Philip	Philippos	("Friend of horses")
Simon	Shimon	("He has heard")
Thomas	Te'oma	("The twin")
Zacharias	Zechariah	("Yahweh remembers")

When Yeshua and His contemporaries talked about God, they avoided using the Hebrew YHWH, as it was considered sacrilegious to use His name openly. In Aramaic, the commonly used word would be Allah, or just using terms like our Father in heaven, The Lord, etc. (The Arabic translation of the Bible uses Allah.)

Chapter 1. December 25 Year 758 AUC.
The Dream.

- "Has your birthday been pleasing?" my mother asked me at bedtime. I had snuffled in under thick woolen blankets, my younger brothers were already sound asleep, Hakob beside me and Joses in his cradle. The oil lamp in the front room spread a yellow light in through the door between the two rooms of our house; the light from outdoors through the small window opening was growing weaker with the night falling. I nodded, and stroking my hair, she continued:

- "You are a big boy now Yeshua, five years old. You will soon start to help your father with mending his tools."

- "Yes", I said, "but Mother, tell me now about your dream about the angel."

It had been our own tradition, my mother Miryam's and mine, to talk about her dream once a year, in the evening of my birthday. I do not remember when she started doing this; she might have done it even before I could speak.

- "Ah yes, my dream...", she started, her eyes looking into the distance, "Before you were born, I and your father had just settled into our new home, this house, and we longed for having a family. Early one morning I dreamt that I awoke, and I was not surprised that I was alone, as I knew your father Yosef had already left for work. But I heard someone in the other room, so I put my robe on and went out. There I met a very tall man, clad in a white tunic, and he said 'Do not be alarmed, dear Miryam. I have a message from Allah, saying that you will give birth to a boy. He will become a king, and he will make everyone free.' And he started to glow, brighter and brighter, until I could only see a white, warm light which was stronger than anything I have ever seen, but which still neither burnt or blinded me. After a moment the light faded slowly, and the man had disappeared."

As we always have done this ritual of ours, I asked
- "What did he mean by king? Will I become the king of Galilee, or where? Old Herodes' sons, they are kings now, will they not continue to rule?"

Mother smiled, patted my head.
- "Of course they will. But you will find your own kingdom, is it not so?"

I sat up eagerly - now it was my turn:
- "Yes, that I have been told in my dreams. In my dreams the angel you met comes and gives me a golden chalice, and he says that this is your weapon. With this you will conquer the world. What does he mean, how can a chalice be a weapon?"

Even though we had played this game many times, there came sadness in my mother's eyes, when she said

- "I do not know, my beloved Yeshua. All the other boys in the village dream of joining the zealots, and they long for learning to fight with swords and daggers. And we never win, many die... Maybe the chalice means that you will fight with words, with new thoughts."

These words were the ones that always had signaled the end of our yearly tradition. All of the times before, I had not understood what she meant, only understood her anxiety and her sorrow, and we had just hugged. But this time, I felt something growing inside, like a fire in my stomach, working its way up.

- "I am going to search for that chalice! I will find it and then I will become a king!"

My mother Miryam looked at me, a surprised look in her eyes. She saw that I did not smile; I was not playing our old game any longer.

- "But how will you know it is the right chalice you find?"

- "I will drink out of it. If it makes me strong I will carry it with me out into the world and I will give others to drink. The ones I give this to drink from will never be thirsty again!"

My mother looked at me in a strange way, almost shocked:

- "I have never told you – the angel in my dream said something like that, but I could never understand what he meant, so I never told anyone. And now *you* say it..."

- "I know it for sure", I said, "I *will* find that chalice."

- "I think you will...", she said, "but now it is time to sleep. Tomorrow early you have to go to the Rabbi with your brother for your reading lessons. I wish you a good night now, my little boy."

And she hugged me, longer than she usually did, and tucked me in.

Chapter 2.   Maius 17 763.
The Angel.

Herodes Antipas had been king of Galilee a couple of years, but there was much unrest in both our country and in Judea, and there had been shortage of food the whole winter. The former large town of Sepphoris, the nearest town to us here in Nazareth, was still in ruins after the Roman sacking.

Our lessons at the Rabbi had been reduced to once a week, as even we younger boys had to work in the fields all day. Except for me, I had an extra reading lesson, as the Rabbi had convinced my father that I had an unusual aptitude for scripture.

But now it was evening, the still and cool hours before sunset. I and my two brothers Hakob and Joses were playing in the yard behind our house. Shimon was inside, helping our mother to watch little Esther that still lay in her cradle.

- "I am Yehudah of Galilee, and you Hakob will be Quirinius!" Joses shouted and rushed towards his elder brother, wood sword over his head.

Hakob clambered up on the stone wall surrounding our house, defending himself with a makeshift shield, using a bucket lid, holding it by its rope handle.

- "I will summon the Emperor's soldiers and I will crucify you all and the dogs will pee on you bones!"

Hakob shouted back, "Yeshua, come help me with this bandit!"

- "You will lose both of you", I said, crossing my arms. "Yehudah will be killed a year from now, and his war will lead to nothing. The Romans will stay for a thousand years. But then the whole Roman Empire will fall as well."

Hakob sank down on the stone wall, sitting with his legs dangling.

- "You and your dreams, Yeshua... But we have Allah on our side, we cannot lose this war! We have the right to the Holy Country. Allah has given us this right. He will not wait a thousand years. So says the Rabbi."

Joses, only five, did not really understand this, but took it as an encouragement:

- "I am Yehudah the Galilee, and Allah is on my side! He will help the zealots in the Holy War!" Again, he threatened Hakob with his sword.

I sat down on the ground, remembering the dream I had the previous night.

- "Last night I dreamt again that the angel spoke to me. He said that those who use the sword to kill will be killed by swords. And he said that those that give life will live forever."

- "Now you are crazier than usual, Yeshua. How can we ever become free if we don't fight?" Hakob exclaimed, jumping down from the wall to sit in front of me. Joses looked disappointed, realizing that the playing had ended, because his two elder brothers started to discuss, as they always did. He sat down at a distance, and started to build a farm on the ground out of the bucket lid and pieces of goat dung.

- "We will never become free as long as we believe this." I said, "I know the Rabbi tells us to believe in the Holy war that will come and free us. All this talk about the Messiah that will lead us to victory. But Mother says that each one that has claimed to be the Messiah, has been killed."

- "Yes, but the Rabbi also warns us about false prophets", Hakob retorted, "and he says that the ones that have been killed have not been the real Messiah!"

I put my hand on Hakob's shoulder and said calmly, with a deep feeling of being completely sure about what I was going to tell him.

- "My angel tells me that the Messiah will be the one that gives life. He will not use the sword, because it will lead to death for everyone."

- "Tell that to the women in our village who have become widows because of the Romans. Tell this to the other mothers who have lost their sons who fought for our rights!" Hakob muttered angrily.

- "You know, Hakob", I said slowly and carefully, "I think I am going to. Not now of course, but somehow I know I will tell them. And I feel frightened, because it will not be an easy telling. Sometimes in the future, I will even tell the Rabbi that he is wrong."

- "You are really crazy, Yeshua" Hakob said, but looked a little impressed at me, shaking his head but at the same time smiling.

Chapter 3.   September 19 764.
The Rabbi.

- "I think you are almost as learned as I, Yeshua my boy. I am really impressed that you find the time to read at home, with all the work you have to do for your father."

The Rabbi sat behind his small desk in the lesser room inside the main room of the synagogue. I sat on a rug on the other side of the desk, carefully holding a Torah scroll in front of me.

We had been talking about what the Torah says about Israel as the holy country given to the Jews from Allah, and about "Milhemet Mitzvah", the mandatory Holy War. I had never revealed to the Rabbi anything about my dreams, but I could not stop myself from asking him questions. My angel's repeated statements about that I would use my Chalice as my weapon had almost become an obsession inside me, something I carried with me always. Every day things happened that made me think of it: the other boys playing the Holy War, the recurrent funerals of young men in our village and in many other villages nearby, my parents' heated discussions late nights.

I could, like everyone else, also feel rage inside towards the Romans, and towards the high priests in Jerusalem that I felt betrayed us, but I could not let go of my Angel's emphatic words on how violence only creates more violence, in an ever increasing vicious circle.

- "And of course you as a young man, already ten years old, have the right to criticize the elders, and the hot-heads of your own age, but you should not criticize the Law…" the Rabbi said. Bending forward, as if to emphasize what he was going to say, he continued:

- "I think if you study Parshat Ki Teitzei more, you will understand that this is something we Jews have thought through in very large depth. If we start to diverge from the Law, we are nothing. What does your cousin Ohannes say about this? He has studied with the Nazarites for two years now."

I knew that I was treading dangerous ground, even if the Rabbi was a very old friend of my family, a person I had known all my life, a person I liked and trusted. But in this I could not help myself: I could not bring myself to accept what the Law said, what everybody said. The night before the Angel had showed me images that had made me wake up, sweaty and trembling: I saw whole Jerusalem burnt to the ground, the Temple in rubbles, and everybody killed, men, women, and children. It had not been an ordinary nightmare, it had felt as if I had travelled there, into the future, and that I had actually seen it, smelled the horrible stench of burned flesh, heard the moanings of the few still living but soon to perish, stumbling around in the ashes. Remembering the dream made my heart beat.

The Rabbi saw my anxiety, and assuming that I had felt intimidated by his reproach, he said

- "But do not take this as I think it is unforgivable to discuss this. It is a good thing that you and I are such good friends, and good friends should be able to reveal their thoughts to each other with trust. What I am saying is that your thoughts about violence only leading to new violence are wise, in all other things than this. In this we have Allah on our side, and we must obey His commandments."

A little relieved about his friendly way of saying this, I asked

- "But even if the Torah says this, and this has been the truth for us during thousands of years, all the time since Moses freed us from the Pharaoh and led us to the Promised Land, how do we *really* know it is Allah's truth? People have believed things thousands of years long before us, things that we now see as superstition and mistakes."

The Rabbi looked at me, seemingly in deep thoughts. He remained quiet a long while, and I again started to feel that I had maybe offended him. But to my relief he said

- "You are right. Many have believed in complete falsehood. Many still do, for example all these false

Messiahs and prophets that wander about and turn peoples' heads around, talking about the end of the world. I believe that if they really followed Allah's commands in what they are doing, they would not be killed. But I still believe that if we keep our heads cool and follow the Law, Allah will show us the way to victory."

I knew deep down, and how I knew this I could not fathom, but I knew that it was just *this*, blindly following the Law, that would lead us to the disaster I had seen in my dream. But I found no way of expressing this, without revealing my talks with my Angel, so I just said

- "I wish all the hot-heads could have your patience, Rabbi. Maybe then they would be able to silence their loud thoughts of revenge, and they would be able to hear Allah's Voice within themselves. But thank you, Rabbi, for this was a good talk. I am thankful for your lending me this valuable scroll, and I will study more, until I understand."

The Rabbi looked surprised, was silent again for a long time, and then sighed:

- "Again, Yeshua, I am amazed that you are only ten years old. You talk like an old soul. Maybe you are... But thank you yourself, our talks really forces me to examine my own thoughts. You are welcome to borrow the scroll as long as you need it, as long as you bring it back here for the services. I know I have kept you here longer than Yosef likes, and I am sure he is waiting now for you to come back and help him mend his tools. So fare well for today, young Yeshua."

Chapter 4.   Aprilis 15 766.
The Temple.

Almost everybody in our village had travelled together to Jerusalem for Passover, as we did every year. Only the very old and the crippled stayed home, and we had provided for them for the coming weeks.

Many had carts pulled by donkeys, but most of us travelled by foot. The pilgrimage to Jerusalem had taken three days, as we dared not travel through Samaria. As always before, we travelled east of Jordan through Perea and then west into Judea, even though the shortest road would have taken almost a day less.

We had now been to the Temple for two days, and I was wandering around for myself in the court of Gentiles, looking at all the people jostling one another in front of all the merchant booths and the money changers. My siblings have stayed with our relatives in the tent camp outside Jerusalem, and my parents were further inside the Temple. My mother was going to make a sacrifice in the Court of Women, and my father and the other elders from our village were going to try to come all the way into the Court of Israelites to participate in a service.

Since I was ten, I had received a small salary from my father for the work hours I then had started to spend together with him in Sepphoris, where many had got building work for Herodes Antipas' new palace and the reconstruction work for the town. I had brought a small sum with me on this year's pilgrimage, and I had now bought a small star pendant in a leather string to commemorate my 'Bar Mitzvah' that I had gone through the day before, the ceremony that signified that I was now an adult member of our community.

With the star on my chest, I did not feel like a mere boy anymore, and I imagined that the children around me looked at me as the grown-up man I felt I now was. The fact that my parents trusted me to wander around by myself like this, and to find my own way back to the tent camp, also felt good.

- "Young King David, what do you think of our temple", a tall Pharisee said smiling at me. "We are honored to have you inspect us like this on Passover proper!"

- "Thank you Rabbi, it is my honor to be here. You have become civilized, and I am relieved that you do not sacrifice virgins to Moloch any longer", I joked back.

The priest looked surprised at my rash answer, and said

- "Would you prefer we did, venerable King?"

- "No, I thinkest sacrifice should be of the past all together. Death does not give us life." I said, hoping he would take it as my continued joking, even if I felt that my words had come from my heart.

- "Lucky for you, my King", the priest said, making himself a seat on merchants' chest, "that a high priest did not hear you. A Sadducee would not take that kindly, even from a king…"

I felt friendliness and warmth from the priest, so even with his words of warning I felt that he was more intrigued than offended. I could feel that the playful interchange of these words had sparked again the fire in my chest. It had again ignited my longing for finding Truth behind all the rituals, all the hundreds of interpretations of the Scripture, all the different schools of thoughts. The Rabbi back home had told me about twenty-four different ones here in Jerusalem only…

- "I have learned that a sick man needs to sacrifice a dove without blemish, cedar wood and hyssop herb. Then after cleansing himself eight days he has to sacrifice again, two lambs this time. After this he is free of sin, but if he remains ill it is his own fault."

- "So you think we do this just to earn money?" the priest said, suddenly looking serious.

- "No, I think you offer these services in good faith. But I believe that sickness comes out from *seeing* oneself sinful, even if one is without sin. And the sacrifices might make the sick man to believe this even more."

The priest looked at me, deep in thoughts. I saw that despite his long beard he was actually quite young, maybe in his thirties.

- "What is your name, and where are you from, my boy? I ask not to threaten you, I ask you because I would like you to follow me to our quarters just inside the passage to the Court of Women. We are a group of younger priests that just have been discussing the interpretation of sacrifice, and it seems to me that you have put some thought to this."

Relieved, curious and also flattered by his invitation, I said

- "I am Yeshua bar Yosef from Nazareth. I had my Bar Mitzvah yesterday, and I am therefore allowed to go where I want by myself. My parents and my brothers and sisters and our relatives are staying at a tent camp north of Jerusalem. I would be glad to follow you, Rabbi. Could I first buy something to eat and drink before I follow you there?"

The priest stood up, smiled and said

- "That will not be necessary, young Yeshua. You will eat and drink as our guest."

He walked towards the entrance to the inner court, making his way slowly through the thick throngs of people, booths, tables, animal cages, and litter. I walked just behind him, my heart beating quicker than before, partly because of the effort to avoid bumping into people, but also because of the anticipation of talking to a group of priests, all by myself.

We washed ourselves at a basin besides the entrance, and I followed him into the Court of Women. On the opposite side of the court I could see the large entrance to the Court of Israelites, and above and beyond the wall rose the high tower of Holy the Holies. The thick stench of burnt meat from the sacrifice altars that kept burning all day almost made me choke, despite the officiating priests' efforts to cover the smell with incense and burning of herbs.

We entered a small room behind a long row of high pillars. Coming from the stark sunlight outside I could at first see nothing, but after a while I could see two priests sitting on wooden stools at a crude cedar wood table in the middle of the room. Around the walls there were open chests with fruit and vegetables, and on iron hooks on the wall besides the entrance raw meat was hanging, covered with flies.

My newfound friend greeted the other two, sat down on a stool and invited me to sit down at the head of the table.

- "This is my friend Yeshua bar Yosef from Nazareth. I have invited him here to share our food, and to talk about how to understand the scriptures. Yeshua had his Bar Mitzvah yesterday, and is a son of the commandment as well as a grownup man that takes care of himself. Oh, and I forgot to say my own name to you, my boy" he said, now turning towards me.

- "I am Nicodemus bar Gurion and I am from here. My family have lived in Jerusalem for four generations. My priest brothers here are Isaac bar Simeon from Jericho and Jason bar Jacimus from Capernaum."

The other priests had also thick black beards, but looked to be the same age as Nicodemus. As I recognized Jason from having seen him a couple of times in Nazareth, where I believed he had relatives, I felt a little less nervous. I greeted them, repeating their names, and said

- "You Rabbi Jason I have seen before, do you not have relatives in my home village?"

- "Yes", he said, looking closer at me, "a first cousin of my mother lives there, Avigail, married to Jonas. But are you not the son of Miryam, cousin to Elisheba in Bethletepha, just recently widow after one of our priests, Zechariah?"

I felt nervous again, not knowing how much of the rumors he had heard, and how he had interpreted them.

- "I am the oldest son of Miryam, cousin to Elisheba. I and my cousin Ohannes, their only son, spend much time together. He is six years older that I and I regard him as an older brother. He is a member of the Nazarite brotherhood and is as learned as any rabbi."

- "And he could have been one", Simeon said, "but the stubborn boy refuses to accept his rightful allowance from the Temple, as a son of Zechariah and as a scholar. A waste to be a mere shepherd; a mind like his would have been like clear water here in this spiritual marchland..."

- "But this explains a lot!" Nicodemus exclaimed, "There is one good example of what I and young Yeshua were talking about before – how beliefs can have power not only over the brain, but also on the body. Not until her dream about the angel Gabriel was she able to conceive, and when this happened she was even far beyond the age where this should have been possible. Not to mention old Zechariah...", he chuckled.

- "We were all of us three here in the Temple when *his* refusal to believe first made him mute, and when they asked him what to name his son, the complete change of his beliefs suddenly gave his speech back again", Jason said excitedly. "But tell me more, Nicodemus, what kind of beliefs were you two talking about before? If this Yeshua is a first cousin of Ohannes bar Zechariah, and has spent time with him, he surely harbors interesting ideas."

- "Well", Nicodemus said hesitantly, "maybe you Yeshua should explain this again, now to all three of us. You said something about that sacrifice might strengthen mistaken beliefs about one's sinfulness, and that death cannot bring new life. Or did I understand you incorrectly?"

And we discussed, and many hours passed quickly. We paused for Simeon to go out and roast some of the sacrificial meat, and Jason brought bread, vegetables and wine to the table, water for me, and we then continued to talk while eating. I felt more and more at home with these three men, despite that they were more than twice my age, were scholars and spoke with many words I did not fully understand. What I did understand after a while was that they opposed both the subservient attitude of the high priests towards the Romans *and* the fanatic approach of the zealots. I gathered that they often between themselves had discussed some kind of middle road.

I even shared my dreams about my Angel with them, and how I more and more had been having "waking dreams" of talking with Him, something I had not before told anyone except my brother Hakob and my cousin Ohannes. When the Pharisees understood the width of my divine conversations, their amused interest in what I think they regarded as a gifted boy with interesting ideas shifted to a serious and at times intense interrogation.

Their questions and comments on what I told them made me think more deeply about things that had become more and more natural to me, and I started even to see my own experiences in a new light, figuratively seeing myself through their eyes.

Among many other things, we talked about the impossibility to make an image of Allah, and that this could be the cause of all the different interpretations of the scriptures. I realized then, that my limited human mind *could* have made up the image of the Angel as a way for my Father to speak to me. Or rather, that the Angel was *one* manifestation of Him, a manifestation that could be experienced totally different by someone else, but that the message would be the same.

We all lost track of time, until we noticed that the sunset had passed, and Nicodemus said

- "Your parents are probably looking for you, but we dare not let you wander by yourself at this time, in the dark. Stay with us tonight, and we will help you to keep an eye for them in the morning."

- "I do not think they are worried yet", I said, "as they told me that if it was too difficult to pass through town, I could spend the night with one of my relatives, that has found roof tents to rent nearby."

And as darkness fell over the Temple, the sounds from the outside abated. Soon I could hear only the sounds from the animals, and I could hear the priests pray silently. They fetched sleeping rugs from one of the crates, and after having washed we soon all slept on the floor.

***

Next day we continued talking, but now not all four of us at the same time, as they had different duties to take care of. Instead, I spent time, sometimes several hours, with one of them at a time. I felt more and more at home with them, and again I lost track of time completely: to my surprise it was suddenly night again, and this time I resolved to leave next morning in order to find my parents, which I suspected now might be wondering.

Next morning again, after having eaten breakfast, our discussions continued, and none of us noticed a rustle at the door. The voice of my father startled me, as he was standing just behind me:

- "In the name of Allah, Yeshua, where have you been! We thought you had decided to live with my cousin as we agreed, and then we thought that you had decided to travel home with him, instead of trying to find us in this mess. But when we had travelled a whole day, and still not found you, we returned, and now I find you here! It does not even seem that you care!"

Embarrassed, I rose, and said

- "Forgive me Father, but these men have become like my elder brothers, and we have been talking about our Father in heaven, in Whose house we are. I felt so at home here that I forgot the time."

Becoming aware of the three priests, it was now my father's turn to become embarrassed, and he seemed even grateful when I introduced him to Nicodemus, Isaac and Jason. They bade my mother to come forward, and they asked my parents to stay and eat before we departed.

When my father and mother had gotten to know the connections with Zechariah, Elisheba and Ohannes, and understood that Jason had relatives in Nazareth, they even started to enjoy themselves and stayed longer than I think they had planned to do when they first found me.

Finally, we warmly bade each other farewell, and I departed from the Temple together with my parents onto our travel north.

Chapter 5.   October 1 767.
Ohannes the Nazarite.

- "I can really understand how you feel", Ohannes said, "it took me a year. In the beginning after my father passed away, the pain in my heart was terrible. I know it may not feel that way now for you, but the pain slowly receded, and for me there is just a tender sadness left now. What also helped me was to think of the full and rich life he had, and to think of the happiness my birth gave him."

- "Yosef my father had also a rich life. But he was not blessed with such a long life as Zechariah had. And you and your father had such strong bonds and such nearness. What pains me most is the tension we had his last six months, and the sorrow I gave him."

Ohannes, my cousin, and his mother Elisheba were visiting us in Nazareth, and he and I sat on a hilltop overlooking the village, in the shade of a large tree. The weather was warm for the season, and we had brought dried meat, bread and water to my own secluded place, a place I often used when I wanted to be alone.

I had not seen Ohannes for a long time, and since then he now had become a full-grown man, nineteen years old. He was unusually tall, and he had let his hair grow long, down to his shoulders, and had a large beard. He was clad in a garment made of crude camel hair cloth, and he wore a leather girdle. He had adopted this style of clothing three years before, after having read about the prophet Elijah on Mount Carmel.

Ohannes sighed and said

- "You were not the one that gave him sorrow, he gave himself that sorrow. He could have accepted that you want another life, instead of trying to persuade you to accept becoming betrothed with Hannah. He could have chosen to accept your word, even if you could not explain why to him."

Ohannes' mentioning Hannah brought back all the memories of the heated discussions I and my father had had, and the tension the whole thing also brought with it between him and my mother and in our whole family and among our relatives. I got so restless that I had to stand up and walk around. Ohannes remained sitting, looking at me. Almost on the verge of crying, I said

- "I *could* have tried to explain about my talks with the Holy Spirit. I *should* have tried to make him understand…"

- "You did try", Ohannes protested, "and remember how you told me the other day how upset he became, even using words like blasphemy, and this though you only indicated indirectly about your close connection with Allah. You forget how dependent Yosef always was of keeping his good relations with the other elders, and how carefully he had to choose his words when the rumors about you were discussed in the village counsel. I do not want to talk badly about Yosef, but in this case he closed both his heart and his ears!"

- "Yes, you are right", I said, feeling a little calmer. I sat down on one of the goat skins we had brought with us. "And I feel that my mother, even if she had never said anything about it, has understood me all the time. I have not talked to her openly about my Angel for a long time, but we share the experience, and when I was a child we often talked about her own encounter."

We sat silent for a while, looking out over the village. It was a beautiful day, nature had started to acquire autumn colors and the air was still. Larks could be heard warbling high up in the sky; they had just come from the north, as the nights had been growing colder.

I continued:

- "We talked the other day, before you and aunt Elisheba came, about how her life was going to be now, widow with six young ones – Rivka is only three. And I told her that I might want to study somewhere else than with the Rabbi. She asked me if I was thinking of joining the Nazarites, like you, but I said that the plans that had come to me were different. I told her I might want to leave home, and that I believed that Hakob with the help of our relatives should be able to manage the responsibility of being the oldest man in the house. When she asked me where to I thought of going, I told her I did not know, but that I was going to talk with you when you came."

- "And here I am", said Ohannes. "So, what are your thoughts about this?"

Not sure how he would take it, him being a Nazarite and having taken the vow, I said slowly

- "I have been thinking of learning of other ways of thinking. I need to come away from the teachings of the Law, I need to be able to see things in a new light…"

- "I know you need this", Ohannes said. He leaned towards me and put his big strong hand on my arm, letting it rest there. "I know that it is in your destiny to make up new teachings."

With a frown, he continued

"I, for one, am in need of new teachings. The vows of the Nazarites of no contact with the dead forbade me to attend my father's burial. I disobeyed, so afterwards I made sacrifice at the Temple, but in my heart I am still disobedient…"

Reassured by his touch and his steady gaze into my eyes, I ventured

- "The Holy Spirit has told me many things that contradict the Law completely. I know in my heart that these things in the Law have been made up by man, and they have been stated for so long time, even thousands of years, that they have become truths that are not allowed to be questioned. But at the same time, I have no words that I can use to change the minds of our people. I need to travel, maybe far away, in order to find these words."

Ohannes smiled and said

- "I have actually been hoping to hear you tell me something like this. As I said, I know deep down that it is in your destiny to come with new teachings, and even if you can only find Allah's Truth in your own heart, you might have to hear it from others before you can listen to your heart. I do not know where this came from, but for my inner eye I can see you travelling to the East, to the sages in the mountains."

I did not at first understand what Ohannes meant by the expression inner eye, but suddenly the notion of inner vision, of seeing another reality within, made me dizzy. I closed my eyes, feeling as if Ohannes' grip on my arm was holding me anchored in the present moment, but also making it possible for me to follow the paths of the future with some kind of inner vision.

I saw myself travelling with a caravan, towards the rising sun. I saw how the path had many crossroads, and for each crossroad I somehow saw where both of the different paths continued. I knew that I would take one of these paths because of decisions I had to make at each of the crossroads in the future. And for my inner eye, I could see where each of these paths led. One led to me returning to Judea, becoming a priest. Other paths led to violent death. Others again led farther away. The tangle of different paths became more and more confusing, the further into the future I followed them, but one thing I could see clearly: from the present moment there was only one path, a path to the East, and I saw that I would start out on that path coming spring.

I opened my eyes, and it felt like I awoke from a lucid dream that had gone on for a long time, but I realized at the same time that only a minute or so had passed.

- "Ohannes, dear cousin. Your words about inner vision opened up something new inside of me. I know now this is something that I have been able to do always, but it has felt too terrifying so I have never dared, I have closed myself to it. Until now: your strength helped me take the step."

And I told him of my vision, about the path I would embark on coming spring, and about how I could see all the different paths possible, far into the future.

Ohannes said, choosing his words slowly and carefully

- "Yeshua, my cousin. We are more than cousins, we are more than even brothers. Allah wills us both to follow the paths given to us. I know that my path is to leave the Nazarites and to form new laws, the laws for the new age. Yeshua, what does your inner vision show about this?"

Ohannes earnest voice and the intenseness of his eyes fixed on me made me feel terrified again of the gift I understood had now awakened in me. How could I, still only in my fourteenth year, take on the responsibility of another person, especially Ohannes, who I always had regarded as wiser than me?

But, his hand on my arm again calmed me, and I closed my eyes, and this time I could at will enter my visions of the future. It felt as if I had been able to do this all my life, without knowing I could. This time I followed Ohannes' path from the present moment, forward in time. Again, I could see the crossroads, the different choices he would have to make, the different paths going from the crossroads farther into the future. I abandoned all paths that ended with his death in the next few years, the deaths so common among prophets and truthsayers in Palestine. Instead I followed a path that I saw would make Ohannes and me meet again, in the far future. It surprised me that I could not see beyond that point, but it also calmed me that the point in time was so far into the future.

I opened my eyes, and said

- "Ohannes, I saw. But I will not tell you all the different things I saw about your life, because most of it will never happen. What will happen, if both you and I make the right choices at the different crossroads, is that you and I will meet again in the far future, and that we will take on different roles in the same mission."

Ohannes tightened the grip on my arm and said eagerly

- "Yeshua, tell me now – what shall I do?

It felt like our roles had changed, like he was the younger, despite being so much larger, and bearded. I felt uncomfortable in this - it went against all I had learnt about respecting my elders. But then I said

- "Ohannes, you shall return home and take care of your mother. With her, and with the work you need to do to support her and yourself, you shall wait for the coming of our Father's hour."

It felt like these words just came out from somewhere deep inside, I had not thought them out, it was as if someone spoke through me. At the same time I knew that I had spoken the truth, and I felt that my advice to my elder cousin was the one he had to follow, for us to meet again in that far future I had envisioned.

Ohannes let go of me and covered his face with his hands. I could see that he was crying. Now it was my turn to take hold of him, and I asked

- "Ohannes, what grieves you?"

Ohannes sighed deeply, looked up at me, and said

- "I am not grieving. These tears are of happiness and relief. Now I *know* that there *is* a mission for me, I know that this is Allah's will for me, and I know that you are His messenger. I trust He will let me know when to take my next step."

We sat looking at each other for a long time, without saying anything more, just taking the time to absorb what had just happened, time to take in the enormity of it, time to think of how different both of our lives would become from this moment on.

Finally Ohannes said

- "We need to go back to our mothers. Let us not talk about this to anyone."

And we rose, packed our things into our shoulder sacks, and we walked together slowly down the hill towards Nazareth.

Chapter 6.   Martius 23 769.
The Essene.

- "Do you miss our former company, Yeshua? We travelled with them for more than half a year. A pity they decided to take the north route after Kabul, and not go to Satavahana."

I and Rabbi Hoshea, my travel companion and guardian, sat outside our tent, looking at the sunset. We had travelled for a month after Kabul, and the caravan leader had announced that we would reach Pataliputra, the capital of Satavahana, in a couple of weeks the weather permitting. Summer had come, and some days were very hot. The new caravan we now were travelling with included both many of the members of our previous one, and many new ones. In all we were almost two hundred travelers.

- "Yes, Rabbi", I said. "It was intriguing to hear them talk about China, from the ones of them that had been there before. I sometimes wish I could have more than one lifetime - there is so much to learn about the world. Having seen just Galilee and Judea, the world is so much larger than I understood when I was younger."

- "There is surely much to learn in China", Hoshea said, "but there you will not find the teachings you need to learn about. Pataliputra is the largest city of the world, and if you want to learn about Veda and Buddha, that is the proper place. Even I, who have lived there before, hope to bring back new scriptures home to B'nai-Amen."

He surely knew what he was talking about - the teachings of the Essenes included much of ancient knowledge from both Hinduism and Buddhism. I had gathered this from the long discussions about my continued studies I had with him while we were still at home. Rabbi Hoshea was in his sixties, but strong as a young man, and he was an Essene from the Nazorean branch. My cousin Ohannes had asked the Rabbi to visit us in Nazareth in order to offer my mother guardianship for me on my trip, and it was Hoshea who had proposed that I should travel to the Satavahana Empire.

- "You were quite open with your thoughts during our stay in Kabul", Hoshea said, then making a pause as if to choose the right words for what he intended to say next. And he continued

- "And that was good at that place, they are eager to learn new things, and it seems like you even got those who thought you were a prophet and wanted to be your followers. But, in Pataliputra it will be different. I have not been there for thirty years, but I am sure it is still the way I remember it. There are four groups of people – castes – that are by the law there obliged to certain rights and certain obligations."

- "Yes", I said, eager to show him that I remembered, "you told me about these back home – the Brahmins, the Kshatriyas, the Vaisyas and the Shudras."

- "What I did not tell you", Hoshea said, "as I did not want to worry your mother, is that the Brahmins are not open at all towards influence from other teachings. They are not as bad as the Sadducees or the Romans, but you will need to be more careful when you come there. Just as in the towns that we have stopped in during this trip, the common people will gladly hear how they can oppose their oppressors, and both the Vaisyas and the Shudras are very limited in what they allowed to do, especially the Shudras."

- "But how do the Essenes handle this? You teach that all men are equal, do not the Brahmins feel threatened by that?" I asked.

- "We Essenes have been in different places here in the East for more than two hundred years. We have secret members very high up, even in the palace of Pataliputra. We never tell anyone outside about this, but I tell you because I know you now. I was not wholly sure before, but after these eight months that we have been together, Yeshua, the knowledge has been growing inside of me as in a mother awaiting her child."

Hoshea turned towards me, and held his hands over his stomach as if to show that what he said was a concrete truth, and he said slowly:

"Yeshua, we Essenes have been waiting for the Mashiakh for many hundreds of years. Everything we do has been a preparation for this Great Avatar to come through us. And the truth that has been growing inside of me, and in many of us at B'nai-Amen, is that you are the One."

Many different things that had happened during the last year fell into place for me, hearing this. Seemingly chance meetings with other Essenes. Things that Rabbi Nicodemus had said at our latest Temple visit over Passover in Jerusalem. Ohannes' involvement in Hoshea's visit to Nazareth. How this trip probably was the result of an intricate plan of the Essenes. How things had probably had been planned for a long time, maybe already at the famous birth of Ohannes, more than twenty years ago.

But, I also felt a great sadness, because I knew that I would have to make him disappointed. I said

- "Many in Palestine have been talking about the Messiah that will come and free them from the Roman oppression. They are talking about a new king of the Jews that will lead them. I am not the one they are waiting for."

Hoshea leaned towards me, and took my hands in his, and said

- "We know you are not. The Mashiakh is not the Messiah they talk about. Mashiakh is the one who will open the gates to heaven for every man on Earth! He is the one who will lead us Essenes in this mission!"

It was as if his touch pulled me into his vision, and I suddenly saw the whole future of the Essenes. I remembered the dream I had five years earlier about Jerusalem burning, and I knew now that the Essenes would perish then as well, and that their teachings and scriptures would disappear and become forgotten. I saw for my inner vision how their teachings would be found again, but not until two thousand years had passed. I had closed my eyes, and I now took a deep breath and opened my eyes again and said:

"Rabbi Hoshea, you have become dear to me, as much as my father Yosef was. It grieves me to crush your hopes and your beliefs, but I am not your Mashiakh either. I know that the path Allah has decided for me will lead me back to Palestine again. And I know that the Essenes will play an important role in the mission Allah will have me pursue. But I am not the one you have been waiting for. He will never come."

Hoshea let go of me, and clenched his hands into fists so hard that I could see his knuckles grow white, and he said hoarsely:

- "How do you know this? You cannot know this! This has been prophesied for so long, and we have seen all the signs building up, first from Zechariah and Elisheba when they got Ohannes, and from your mother Miryam's encounter with the angel Gabriel. We have been observing you since you were born!"

I felt deeply sorry for him, as I had made his dream crumble. I knew what I had now said would make many thousands of dreams crumble. I said:

- "I know it. But I can also say that you are not completely wrong. I *will* open the gates to heaven for every man and woman on Earth, but it will not happen as you have thought. Allah has revealed my path only up to the point when I return, but I know where the path is heading. And I know that the Essenes will play an important role in this plan. And that you, Hoshea, are playing an important role in my life just now."

The Rabbi leaned backwards on the tent pole behind him. His shoulders sagged and he closed his eyes. He breathed out at length, as if he had been holding his breath. And he said quietly, almost talking to himself:

- "Just as the becoming mother does not know anything about the child she is bearing, I did not know. I knew that a Truth was growing inside, and I know that this Truth has now come out. And just as the mother is happy looking at the new-born child, completely disregarding the gender or the color of the hair, I am happy to have received the Truth."

The sight of him, and hearing his words, moved me to tears, and I said:

- "Rabbi Hoshea, I love you for your open heart, for your open mind and for your wisdom. I am really longing for you to show me the secrets of the teachings ahead. And I am so thankful to have gotten you at my side."

He looked at me, and smiled:

- "It is I who shall be thankful. I am really longing for hearing more about your Truth, and longing for how you will come to understand it yourself even more."

And with this the tension of the moment abated, and we were after a while talking about the days ahead, of what would happen in Pataliputra, and practical issues, as we so often had done during this voyage. When the sun had disappeared behind the hills to the west, we prepared for the night and went to sleep inside our tent.

Chapter 7.   Sextilis 14 774.
The Shudra.

- "Master Issa, I need to talk to you at once!"

My friend Kumara came running into my and Rabbi Hoshea's quarters. Kumara was the leader of a group of Shudras that had formed a secret community for learning about Allah from us.

- "Dear Kumara, my friend. What is the rush, we are to meet this afternoon. The Rabbi is waiting for me at the library in the palace, can it wait?" I said.

- "No, no, master Issa. This is really urgent – we have talked to some friends which are Vaisyas, they work with book-keeping for the White Priests, and there is a plot for your life."

My stomach turned into a knot of fright, and I could first not think clearly. I stood up, walked to the window and looked out on the street below, bustling with people, cattle, elephants, market booths.

We had been here in Pataliputra for five years, and we had never felt threatened. In the beginning, I had been presented by Hoshea as a theological student wanting to learn about the religions of the East, and I had no difficulties to stay in this role – on the contrary, the first years I had to devote all my time to learn Sanskrit and to study the Hindu and Buddhist Sutras.

But after a time, my discussions with the White Priests had raised many questions in me, questions I did not ask them openly, but which I could discuss more freely in the growing group of Shudras that we met with.

After a moment, I managed to calm myself, and I said

- "Why should they want me out of the way – I have not challenged them in any way. I cannot think of anyone among the Brahmins I know that could harbor such hate for me. I even regard many of them as my friends."

Kumara held both of his hands up, palms towards me, and said

- "Oh no, I do not want you to think badly of your friends. They are not the ones plotting, I think it might even be one of them that let this be known to us, by hidden channels. The Swami and his group are plotting, together with the King's Sachivas, and the message we got was that something was going to happen already the day after tomorrow, after the noon Puja at the Palace Temple."

- "Are they thinking of arresting me", I asked, "in open daylight? Are they not afraid of causing a riot? As it is now in the city, not much will be needed to ignite the anger of people."

- "We suspect that they are plotting to pay people to create a riot against foreign influence, which then makes it possible for them to state that they have to protect you with soldiers, and bring you to the Palace. And after that they will spread an invented story that people can believe, a story of how you have instigated rebellion. And then they will execute you, showing all what happens if you create trouble."

I sat down again at my writing desk, and asked Kumara so sit down as well.

I asked him:

- "What should I do to avoid this threat, do you think, Kumara? Should I go and talk to them, together with my Rabbi, and make them understand that I have no intentions of causing trouble?"

Kumara shook his head vigorously, and said

- "No, it is not what *you* do or say that is the problem for them. It is what *we* do. Your ideas that every man and woman are equal in the eyes of God has changed us, changed our view on the world. Many of us have even started to question the caste system. One of us has secretly started to study Veda and the old history, though we are not allowed to, and he has told us that the castes were invented one thousand years ago by invaders from the north, as a way of maintaining their power over us."

- "Yes, I recognize that pattern", I said, suddenly feeling weary of the ways of people in power all over the world. "In my country the invaders let us have our temples and our faith, as long as we pay taxes to them. But if we object, they kill without hesitation..."

Kumara insisted:

- "Master, it has gone too far, there is nothing you can do, and I think they realize this, else they would just try to bribe you into leaving. They need to make you into an enemy of the kingdom, to scare us into obedience."

- "Then I should do what is safest to your group", I said, "and just announce that I have finalized my studies, and prepare our travel home..."

Kumara interrupted me:

- "No, no, master Issa, that is too late! You need to flee for your life, both you and Rabbi Hossa, already tomorrow night, when it has become dark enough for us to help you safely out of the town. The White Priests have spies in many places, and you will not be able to do this by yourselves. We have contacts and safe detours. Out in the countryside we are just now preparing horses, food and all you need to travel. Tomorrow night, and you cannot bring anything with you!"

Many different emotions stirred up inside me: I felt moved by their love and concern for us, and impressed by all their preparations. I felt intrigued about what the next step in my voyage would be. And I felt sadness over having to leave these people with their dreams. Dreams that would surely not become fulfilled in a long time. I felt guilt for having exposed these people to danger – I could have foreseen this, using my gift of prescience. But I also knew how I most of the time avoided using this gift, as life loses its freshness when you know. Knowing makes one preoccupied with the future, and one loses contact with one's free will.

But now I closed my eyes, and I willed to see my future after tomorrow. I saw myself sitting high up above the clouds, in an ancient house built of giant stone slabs. I saw I would learn one more new language again, and I would learn one more new way of thinking again. I would be there a long time, and my understanding would deepen.

- "You are leading us on a way towards the mountains in Nepal", I said, "to a place where peace resides, to Muktinath where Shakyamuni the Enlightened lived."

Kumara looked as in shock, staring wildly at me, and almost shouted:

- "Who told you? We have not told this to anyone!"

I smiled and said

- "My father holds his hand over me, and He leads you to fulfil his plans. The time has come for the next stepping stone on my path. Everything happening is for our own good."

Kumara knelt before me, lowering his head until his forehead touched the floor.

- "Master Issa, you are an Enlightened already, you have passed the last stone. I am not worthy to stand up in your presence."

I knelt down on the floor in front of him, took him by the shoulders, and raised him up again. I embraced him and said:

- "Kumara. Do not worship me. I deserve your respect for my devotion for you. I deserve your love for the love I feel for you. But you should love me as you love an elder brother. What I can do now, every man and woman will be able to do in the future, and more, when the gates to heaven open, and they awaken from the bitter dream this world is."

Kumara looked bewildered, overcome by conflicting emotions, but after a while he started to smile happily:

- "Issa, my brother. It feels strange to say so, but it feels good. And it feels true. Let me at least feel awe about how far you have come, and about that you will come even farther towards the truth."

I said
- "Brother Kumara, reserve your awe to our Father, who holds His hands over both of us. The only difference between you and me is that I have travelled farther on my path. But you are on the same path.

Our time together here and what you have learnt will help you and your people to continue walking this path."

We both stood up again and looked in silence upon each other. Finally Kumara shook his head, as if to free his mind of everything going on inside, and he said

- "But again, master Issa… Brother Issa. This is the most important thing just now: do not prepare anything, do not start to pack things, do not change your plans for today or tomorrow. If you do it will only raise suspicions. Tomorrow night, one hour after sunset, I and others will come here, and you will follow us. Remember: no sacks, no bags, just the clothes you wear just now!"

We hugged each other one more time, and Kumara rushed away, as hurriedly as he had come.

Chapter 8. Ianuarius 1 780.
Full vision.

- "Master Issa. You have been with us for six years, and we have learnt many things from each other. You speak Pali very well. You have passed all the levels of Dharmavinaya, and you have ascended the vehicle of Bodisattvayana. We believe that you are not far from the final awakening. We have thought and hoped you would stay with us."

My temple brother, the old Lama Devapala, retired abbot of Muktinath, and I sat on thick furs on the floor in the small tower meditation chamber in the Muktinath mountain temple. Through the small window slits we could see both mountain peaks and water falls. One could see why the locals called this place "The Hundred Waters". Far below one could see the main temple in the mountain pass.

- "Khensur Devapala", I answered, "my years with you have given me the greatest learning in my whole life. And I have experienced a peace and a closeness to you who live here, as I have never experienced elsewhere. If it was up to me I could not be happier if I could end my days here. But it is not up to me."

The old Lama nodded and smiled. Then he grew serious again and asked:

- "Is it because of what the travelers told us, about the sufferings of your people in Palestine? I could not understand everything they said. Did they tell you anything specific that has made you come to this decision? Was there a message for you from home?"

- "No Khensur", I answered, "there was no message through them, although I admit that hearing about how much worse it has become back home saddened me, and maybe has contributed some to my decision to travel home."

I paused, thinking about how to select my words. Devapala was a very close friend, a person I trusted completely, the wisest person I had met in my entire life. But, I knew that what I was going to say would stay here, it would be discussed among the brothers, and it would be documented in their scriptures. So it was important that I could make him understand.

- "I have had visions", I started carefully, "visions of the future."

Devapala nodded:

- "Yes, I know, we have talked many times about these. What did your visions tell you this time?"

- "This time", I said, "they have been different from all visions I have had before. I have told you about the first one, when I was thirteen years old, and about others after this. They all included many different possible paths, and I could see how different choices led to different paths. The longest path, the one I have been traversing up to now, led here, and from this point there were before many different paths again. One of them led back to Palestine, where I was to meet again with my cousin Ohannes."

The Lama turned his hands with his palms up, and said:

- "So there are still different choices to make."

- "No", I said, "there is now but one choice, to follow the one path left or not. In my latest vision there was only one path, and this time it continued farther than any of my previous visions have shown. This path leads to the end of my physical life, not far into my future. Just seven years."

The Lama looked intensely at me. He asked sternly:

- "And how do you know that what you have seen is not Maya on your Samsara?"

I smiled, and said:

- "Khensur Devapala, my beloved brother. The vision showed me that *everything* here is Maya. In the vision, my Father told me that nothing here has any meaning by itself. The only meaning there is to anything we do, is what we use it for. If we use it *only* to meet our earthly needs, we will stay in Maya, which is without meaning and has no worth. But, if we use it *also* to awaken and to help others awaken, then it has meaning. The path I have before me is one that will show anyone willing to listen how to awaken to the real world, where there is no suffering and no death."

Lama Devapala closed his eyes, and asked quietly:

- "And what is it that you will do?"

- "I will travel back, and during the trip I will sow seeds, speaking to people. Many of these seeds will end up on rock and will never grow. Others will take root but come among thistles and the small plants will suffocate. But a few will come in fertile soil and will take root and will grow into large trees.

When I come to my country I will first follow brother Hoshea to stay with the Essenes, then I will join with the group led by my cousin Ohannes, and we will then each of us separately sow many more seeds, all around the country. Because of this, the high priests and the Romans will feel threatened, and we will both be killed, Ohannes first, I second."

The Lama opened his eyes and looked at me, tears trickled down his wrinkled cheeks. He remained quiet a long time, then he said with a muffled voice:

- "And there is no other path in your vision?"

- "No", I said, "there is no other path, because this is the One Path. In this physical existence I cannot express in words, neither can I show in action, what the Truth is. No one can. But what I will say, and what I will do, will *point* at Truth, so people become able to find it themselves. But do not be sad, brother Devapala, I said the path leads *to* my physical death. It does not end there."

He looked surprised, stared at me and exclaimed:

- "What did you see more?"

- "I will become my true Self, which is Spirit. As such, I can choose to show myself to the ones still in Maya. In my vision, I saw me showing myself in the body I occupy now, first to the twelve disciples I will have asked to follow me, then to the rest of my followers. I will demonstrate in a way that no one can misunderstand, that death is part of Maya, it is utter illusion. When I have shown this to them, their eyes will open, and they will spread this message over the entire world."

The old monk stood up, his hands trembling. He said, slowly, as with real effort:

- "But … if what you say is true … then you are an incarnation of Shakyamuni, a Buddha!"

- "Yes", I said calmly, "I am one. But I am not to be revered. I am no different from you, no different from anybody. By the Will of my Father, I am just far ahead of everyone else on Earth just now."

- "And if what you say is true, your death is not a sacrifice."

- "No", I smiled, "it is not. It will be painful, and I will probably be weak at times and regret that I walked into this with open eyes. But, no, it is not a sacrifice. My death and my resurrection *is* the message."

The lama sat down again on his fur and folded his legs underneath himself, as if to enter a meditation, and said:

- "Bodisattva Issa. We need to talk more about this, much more. But for now I cannot absorb more. I need to contemplate a while, in order to learn what I am to do with what has been revealed to me. Will you join me?"

I nodded, and placed myself in Lotus Position as well, and closed my eyes. We sat quiet for a long time. I used this time to focus on the present moment, relieving myself a while from the terrible burden of prescience. I felt the Divine energy in everything, the Power out of which we as Divine Beings have built up the material universe from what to our physical senses seems to be emptiness.

Resting in this Presence, I sank down into a complete Inner Peace in being One with my Father.

After a long time, I slowly opened my eyes again. I saw that time, as usual in my meditations, had passed unnoticed by me – it was already dusk, and the sky had turned into a deep blue; the first stars could be seen through the eastern window slits.

The old monk had lit an oil lamp, and he sat looking at me. He said:

- "I thank you for helping me become more awake than I have ever been. I know that what you have seen is the Truth. And I know I have experienced something that no one before me has ever experienced: *meeting* with Truth. You are not only speaking about Truth, you *are* Truth. But as you say, it cannot be conveyed in words. But it will remain in my heart."

- "I love you", I said, "but not only as a brother monk, or as the father you have been to me here. I love you for the Eternal Spirit that you are, one with me and one with our Father."

- "I feel this love", Devapala said, "and I love you the same way. And this love shows me that this is the Power of Awakening. The power that will help everyone to look with new eyes at his fellow man as his brother or sister.

This Power is Compassion and Love, and we need not learn it, but we need to find it within."

- "But", he continued, "I said that I would contemplate on what to *do* about this. As long as we remain in this universe of matter, we have to act concretely. Firstly, we need to prepare your and master Hossa's travel home. That will take a couple of weeks, before everything is arranged. This is good, because I will also need to talk with you about what I shall note in our scrolls. Having had a Boddisattva living here must be recorded properly. But, I think that what you have revealed about your path and your physical death, I would prefer to omit. The risk for misunderstanding is too great."

I felt so grateful for Lama Devapala's combination of great wisdom and his down-to-earth practicality, and I laughed and hugged him.

- "I trust you to write this well. And thank you for your wisdom, your part in all this has been of unmeasurable worth. But now, let us go down and join the others in the evening meal."

- "Yes", he answered, "let us do so. We have actually planned to celebrate the first day in your calendar by treating you with special food today, and we have even saved some of the wine the travelers gave us."

Slowly, not to stumble in the falling dusk, we treaded the narrow path down to the mountain pass, chatting as the old friends we were about this and that.

Chapter 9. December 27 783.
The Baptist.

- "I think, Ohannes", I said, "that the time has come for me to be baptized."

We sat outside Ohannes' tent in a large desert camp, near Bethabara just east of Jordan. I had joined him when he with all his followers passed Qumran on their way north. Four months earlier, I had travelled from Nazareth to be with Hoshea again, and to stay with the Essenes in Qumran, where I had spent time studying their large script collection.

- "You!" he said, a questioning look on his face, "You have been helping me baptize thousands. Why should I, who am not as near our Father as you are, baptize you? It is *you* who should baptize *me*. I know now for sure, what I have known in my heart my whole life I think, that you are the true Messiah. People call *me* that, but I tell them that after me will come one whose sandals I am not even worthy of lacing."

I rose from where I was sitting and sat down on his rug. I put my arm over his shoulders and said

- "Ohannes, my dear cousin. My spiritual brother. We have talked about this many times. I know you still believe that your role in all that is happening is to prepare the way for the Messiah you believe will come, the Messiah that will free our people from the Romans, and who will create a new Israel."

- "How can I believe otherwise", Ohannes exclaimed, "when the prophecies confirm all the signs! The scripture says: The days are coming, declares the Lord, when I will raise up for David a righteous Branch, a King who will reign wisely and do what is just and right in the land. In his days Judah will be saved and Israel will live in safety."

- "One sees what one believes", I said, "and this is something so many believe and have believed for such a long time. But I need to tell you again, there is never going to be such a Messiah. I am the Awakener and I need not create a new world, because the world I speak of already exists, in our hearts. But you have an important role in preparing the way for the Awakener. People see you as a holy man, and you see me as even holier. The truth is that we are all *equally* holy!"

Ohannes was quiet for a long time. Then he turned his head, looked me into the eyes and said

- "But that you are holy, that is a truth you cannot take from me."

- "No Ohannes", I said, "but I want you to see the *whole* truth: as I am holy, the True Son of Allah, so are you. And so is every person on Earth, Yews and gentiles alike."

- "How can the Romans be sons of Allah!" Ohannes cried. "A true Son of Allah does not sin, he does not violate the Holy Commandments!"

- "Sin", I said slowly, to make my word sink in, "does not exist else than in our judgment of our brothers and sisters. Sin would be hurting our Father, and He cannot be hurt. We make mistakes, sometimes horrible mistakes. But if we cannot forgive even the most horrible mistake, we can never help our brothers and sisters awaken to who they truly are."

- "But the ones making these mistakes, as you call it, they should still repent!" Ohannes retorted angrily.

I stood up again, and stretched my back, which had become stiff from sitting, and I said:

- "If you by repent mean regret, I agree. As long as they are righteous, and make up reasons to defend their destructive actions, they cannot regret. And if they cannot regret, they cannot neither forgive themselves nor accept forgiveness from others. And if they cannot forgive themselves, they cannot awaken."

- "And how would they ever do all this?" Ohannes asked with contempt. "How can we ever make them do this?"

- "The *only* way is forgiveness. I you forgive your brother truly, this means that you see him as sinless, and you see upon the evil he may be doing doing as the mistake it is. And that you see that he is keeping himself in bondage by being righteous. The only thing I feel when I see someone imprisoning himself is compassion."

- "We are warriors of different kinds, you and I", Ohannes said, but with a smile. "You fight with love, I fight by trying to shake people into awakening."

- "This is as it should be", I said, "that we have different roles in the mission you and I both are fulfilling. But I tell you, Ohannes, that if you do not let go of your judgment of others, you may bring suffering onto yourself."

What I had seen in my visions, about Ohannes future's different possible paths, had made me sad and frustrated – if I only could make him understand.

- "Be as it will, whatever will happen, will be the will of Allah", Ohannes muttered.

- "It is and is isn't", I said, "because it is also His will that we have a free will and that we make our own choices. If we could not do this, we would never learn and we would never be able to awaken. But then again, He will make us encounter the same choice again and again, until we have learned our lesson."

- "This is something you may have learnt in the East", Ohannes said, "and which I cannot believe – that we may live many lives, and by this we meet these same lessons over and over again. I think we have this one life, this one opportunity, and if we do not repent, that will be it! The end is near!"

- "Let us not argue about this", I said gently, "this is even more complicated than I think you understand.

We will live many lives only as long as we believe in it. As for me, I have awoken even from this belief, and this life will be the last one I live here on Earth."

- "What you are talking about is beyond my ability to understand, Yeshua. But you are right – let us not argue. I feel that on some level we agree. But again, why do you want me to baptize you?"

I sat down again in front of him, and said

- "Because you are Ohannes the Baptist. When people see you baptizing me it will be a signal for our Mission to take form. I also need this signal myself, as a message to some unclear parts in my soul that still lingers in darkness, and that still are unclear of my Mission."

- "Do *you* have unclarity within you?", Ohannes asked, looking skeptical. "I thought that your thoughts, being so clear, provokes the Adversary."

- "The Adversary, like sin, does not exist either", I explained patiently. "The belief in the Devil is something man since the beginning of time has made up, so that he would not have to see his hidden beliefs within himself. We all have a hidden part within our soul that has led us into having mistaken thoughts, which then make us behave without love."

- "So by me baptizing you, we will scare the Devil out of you?" Ohannes asked, smiling at his own joke.

- "Yes", I said earnestly, "if you with the Devil mean my unclear thoughts I may still have about myself. I need to be a chalice containing only pure water."

- "And how will this happen just by me baptizing you?", Ohannes asked.

- "It will not happen because of the Baptism in itself", I said, "but as I said, the Baptism will be a signal both to others and to myself. After the baptism I will wander out into the desert east of here and be with myself, alone with my thoughts, just as you did a long time ago. And I will stay there until all mud in the clear water of my thoughts is gone."

- "I hear that this is something Allah has planned for you, and I am humbled that I may have a role in this", Ohannes said solemnly. "When will be the time for this?"

"A fortnight from today", I answered, "and I would like you to also send a messenger to Nazareth, as I know my eldest brother Hakob and my youngest brother, Yehudah, wish to be baptized as well."

Ohannes and I continued to talk about this the rest of the evening. He accepted most of what I had said to him, but could still not fully accept that the Messiah would never come.

Before we retired into our tent, Ohannes had seen to that one of his disciples would travel to Nazareth the next morning.

Chapter 10. Ianuarius 13 784.
The Desert.

The hour of my Father had come, and I stood on the eastern shore of Jordan together with my mother Miryam and my brothers Hakob and Yehudah. They had arrived to Ohannes' camp late the night before.

We had not seen each other for a whole year, so we had talked with each other the whole morning. Hakob, being twenty-eight, looked the same, but my youngest brother Yehudah had grown into a man since I last saw him, he was now eighteen.

We had talked about Nazareth and about our relatives, but mostly we had talked about Ohannes and the big attention his preaching and his talk about becoming born anew had got all over Palestine. Miryam declared herself content to watch her sons becoming baptized, but she was as excited as Hakob and Yehudah about what would happen soon.

Making our way through the thick throngs of people, tents, cooking fires, and traveling equipment, we came nearer where Ohannes stood out in the water. When we approached, we could hear his strong voice as he pulled a person up from the water, where he just had immersed the man completely:

- "I hereby baptize you, Jason bar Jacimus from Capernaum, and you will from this day be newborn in the eyes of Allah!"

I recognized the name, and I soon saw that it was the Jason I had met in the Temple, more than twenty years earlier. Despite soaking wet, he looked the same, although with many gray hairs in his beard and at his temples. When he came wading nearer the shore, he caught sight of us, and he recognized my mother first, then he looked at me:

- "Yeshua! You are here! I heard that you had joined with your cousin Ohannes the Baptist, and I hoped so to meet you here."

We hugged, he greeted my mother, and I introduced my brothers and him to each other. We walked away from the din around Ohannes, in order to be able to talk without having to raise our voices. He still worked at the Temple, but said that he now had plans to retire, and to move back to Capernaum. He had heard about my trip to the East and was anxious to hear about this, but I said

- "Jason, dear friend. It is time for me now to get baptized, and after this I have to leave at once, but I promise you, I will visit you in Capernaum soon."

- "Yeshua. Last time I saw you, you were already wise. Now I long to take part of how your wisdom has grown even more. Look at you – just thirty and already more far-travelled and experienced than anyone I have ever met! But you are not only to visit, I invite you to come live with me, and if you have company I will have room in my house for them as well."

I thanked him warmly, we hugged again, and I turned back towards the shore with my mother and my brothers.

Coming nearer, we could soon hear Ohannes' voice again, and the din had abated, as he had made a break in the baptizing, and he stood in the water talking to the people. As we came within hearing more clearly, he could be heard saying

- "…the ax is already at the root of the trees, and every tree that does not produce good fruit will be cut down and thrown into the fire."

A man in the crowd asked

- "Master, what should we do then?"

Ohannes answered

- "Anyone who has two shirts should share with the one who has none, and anyone who has food should do the same."

A man clad as a tax collector raised his voice and asked

- "I have the hated work of collecting taxes for the Romans. Will I be punished for this in heaven? What should I do?"

Ohannes said

"Do not collect any more than you are required to."

A soldier asked

- "We are not any more loved than he. What should we do?"

To which Ohannes replied

- "Do not extort money and do not accuse people falsely. Be content with your pay."

Now Ohannes caught sight of me and said with a loud voice:

- "Here comes he who comes after me but who has surpassed me because he was before me! He is the one who should have baptized me, and he does not baptize in water, as I do. He baptizes in the Holy Spirit and in fire."

I answered, in the same loud voice:

- "I am the same as everyone else here. We are all Children of Allah. As a brother, I wish to start anew today, and be baptized together with my brothers and sisters. But before me, baptize my two younger brothers here!"

And I let Hakob and Yehudah pass me, and Ohannes baptized both, after each one had risen from the water again exclaiming:

- "I hereby baptize you, Hakob bar Yosef from Nazareth, and you will from this day be newborn in the eyes of Allah!"

- "I hereby baptize you, Yehudah bar Yosef from Nazareth, and you will from this day be newborn in the eyes of Allah!"

Dripping wet, they came to me and we embraced each other. I said quietly to them:
- "Take care now of our mother. I will leave you now, to meet myself in the desert. We will meet again in Nazareth."

And with this, I waded towards Ohannes, who without hesitation took me by my shoulders and immersed me deep into the water. His hands still on my shoulders, I stood up and looked upwards. It felt as if the water had cleansed my thoughts completely. It was now completely quiet around, so Ohannes did not need to shout this time when he said:

- "I hereby baptize you, Yeshua bar Yosef from Nazareth.
You are Allah's firstborn, His beloved Son.
Master, be on your way, and let it become fulfilled."

I could feel the old fire ignite in my stomach, and I could feel how it spread upwards. It was not burning, it was a fire of light, and I suddenly remembered my mother's words from my childhood: 'A white, warm light which is stronger than anything I have ever seen, but which still neither burns nor blinds'.

I turned towards the people, who stood utterly still and silent, all looking at us, me and Ohannes. I could see the same light flowing from out of each one of them, as if all hearts were stars, shining with a silent light.

I waded slowly to the shore, and when I came up on dry ground, people made silently way, and I walked past them. I picked my mantle up and put my sandals on. Without looking back, I walked out eastwards, out into the desert.

I slowly walked all day, and when night fell, I slept under some trees, as I had not yet reached the desert.

***

The day after, I arrived at the desert. I found a small creek, drank my fill, and continued eastwards, out onto the sand dunes.

During the following days I wandered aimlessly around. Sometimes there was a light rain, and I could find water to drink in small puddles on stony ground. The nights were sometimes cold, and I swept my mantle tightly around myself. During the stay with Ohannes I had learnt which roots and leaves I could eat, and how to find the longhorned grasshopper of the Jordan Valley, one of the few edible insects available here.

But, despite getting to drink and eating a little, I quite soon became very hungry and thirsty. After many days more this became worse and worse, until there was a constant cramping pain in my stomach, and I had to walk bent forward to relieve the pain some.

The thought came:

- "If you are The Firstborn Son of Allah, you have created all this. If you so wished, the stones here on the ground could be turned into wheat bread."

At this thought, I could clearly feel the scent of new-baked bread, and the saliva glands in my dry mouth hurt when in vain trying to produce moisture.

But my constant fire within turned into anger, and I answered the voice within, with loud voice:

- "If I eat of this bread it will become real to me, and I will be trapped!

Man needs not only bread to be alive,
since true life is of the spirit."

***

And I continued my aimless wandering, many hours each day. In the nights the sky was clear, and the nights were therefore very cold. One night it was colder than it had been other nights, and despite my thick mantle I shuddered, and the thought came:

- "If you are The Firstborn Son of Allah, you have created all this. If you so wished, there could be a warming fire here, a fire that never dies down."

And I could feel the wonderful warmth from some invisible source, as if someone had concealed a hearth among the stones around me.

But as before, a white fury arose within, and I answered the voice:

- "If I warm myself at this fire, it will become real to me, and I will be trapped! Man's true warmth is Love, and he needs nothing else to keep warm."

***

After many days I reached a ridge of mountains. I had seen them many days in the east, growing higher and higher each day.

I was now quite weak, and I used a branch I had found to support myself. I entered a valley, where the slope led up to a pass in the high mountains before me. It took me several days to reach the pass, and from there another whole day to reach the summit of one of the mountains. When I reached it, it had already grown almost dark, and I found a shallow cleft that gave some protection from the cold wind, and I could sleep there a couple of hours. I awoke early dawn, freezing cold, dizzy and weak with hunger.

Slowly, I climbed up the last part, and stood on the peak, looking at the sun rise above the eastern horizon. It felt like I saw the whole world spread out before my feet, way below. I could see the sun be reflected in distant creeks and ponds, I could see the edge of the desert, with forests and farm lands beyond.

The thought came:

- "If you are The Firstborn Son of Allah, you have created all this. If you so wished to be down there without having to struggle so, you could just throw yourself down, and Allah's Angels would protect you and bring you safely down. Your divine visions have told you that you will not die now, and you know that these visions are true."

Starting to know this voice well, I knew I could just answer it and it would give up. I did not feel as angry as before, but never the less I answered the voice within:

- "If I allow myself to be tempted to test my powers, I will use them on what does not exist, and my powers will make me believe I *am* Allah, and I will be trapped again.

If Allah wants me somewhere, He will bring me there."

But, this time the voice did not give up as before. Suddenly I could see myself standing before me, floating in the air above the deep precipice in front of my feet. The other me was clad in a blindingly white tunic, with beautiful golden braids along the hem of the mantle. His hair was combed in long curls, his eyes shone with gentle appreciation and with a soft but clear and loud voice he said:

- "You are the Firstborn Son of Allah. You have divine powers over your brothers and sisters, and you can create your kingdom. Everything you see from here will be yours. You are vigilant for your divine purpose here, and this kingdom of yours will last longer than the Romans!"

I answered him in cold fury, slowly, one word at a time:

- "If I create a kingdom on Earth, I and everybody else will be trapped in suffering and death.

I am vigilant only for the True Kingdom of Allah which you know nothing of.

In all your splendor you are but death and nothingness!"

At these words he shrank and he became smaller, younger, until there stood a trembling little boy, near me, at the lip of the precipice. He looked so frail, that a wind gust could well throw him over the edge, and make him fall down to his death, hundreds of cubits below.

- "I don't want to die..." he sobbed.

Seeing him, my heart was filled with compassion and love, and I said:

- "You know nothing because you are only a child. Come to me and I will protect you."

And I took him in my arms, and he cuddled against my chest, I could feel him relax. I heard a deep sigh from him, and he returned in, inside of me. And a thought came, strong and clear, and I knew that this was not a thought of my own making:

- "Nothing real can be threatened.

Nothing unreal exists.

Herein lies the peace of God."

***

After this, the voice never returned. Despite feeling exhausted, dizzy of hunger, my lips cracked bleeding as I had found no water for many days, I felt a profound sense of inner peace, a peace so deep and silent as I had never felt it before.

I returned westward, and walked as fast as my declining strength allowed. The weather had turned cloudy, so the nights were not as cold as before, and I could more often find water to drink, but the grasshoppers seemed to have disappeared, so I was weak of hunger.

After many days I finally reached the forest west of the desert again, and I could there find some edible roots again. Despite this, I was so exhausted I could barely walk, with utmost effort I took one step at a time. My progress was slow, and at times I was not even sure that I walked in the right direction.

I never despaired, though, as the vision of my Mission stayed clear in my mind, and during long periods of time I must have walked blindly, totally inside my visions of the future.

I completely lost track of time, and days and nights passed, as if the sun had begun to fly faster over the sky. I heard voices, and first I thought the inner voice had come back, and my heart started to pound. But I managed to open my eyes, and saw men approaching. I recognized their crude clothing, and knew then that they were from Ohannes' camp. In my relief, my last strength drained, and I fainted.

Chapter 11. Februarius 28 784.
The Mission commences.

- "You were gone forty days", Ohannes said. "You have been out there often in the past, did your weakness make you lose the way?

I had awoken the day before, and had found myself in Ohannes' tent. I was still there now, lying on several thick rugs, with two furs on top of me. Despite this I was freezing. The absence of thirst and hunger was a relief, but I felt so weak I could not even raise my head to look at Ohannes, who sat at the tent opening, looking out.

- "No, I found my Way", I answered, "I found the way to myself out there. But sometimes you have to travel far to realize that you have remained at the same place you always have occupied."

- "Well, now you really have to occupy the same place", Ohannes answered wryly, "you are too weak to do anything else than stay here and let us feed you. You were unconscious the first four days here, we were not sure if you would survive."

- "Thank you, Ohannes, my brother in the spirit, for your care. And for finally setting me off on my Path", I said. "When I am back on my feet, I will be on my way."

Ohannes came over and sat down beside me, and said, brows knit:

- "I thought we were going to preach together, that we are on the same Mission, the one our Father has given us."

- "We are on the same Mission, Ohannes", I answered, "but this Mission requires us, you and I, to go to different places."

- "Well, I know *I* have to leave at least", Ohannes said, "there have been more and more of Herodes Antipas' soldiers here, posing questions, after you left. What happened here when I baptized you has given rise to many stories. Some of these I have heard, and though many are truthful, many sound more like myths of sorcery and magic. And many of these stories point me out as the promoter of the new kingdom of the Jews, despite my understanding now that your goal is a change of peoples' minds rather than a change of government. Many have even asked if I am the new Messiah or if I am Elijah that has returned."

- "In my visions of what may happen, and listen to me, Ohannes", I pleaded, "what *may* happen, I have seen that you are in danger from Herodes Antipas. I think you should leave Judea and Perea and go south. When I have regained my strength, I will travel back north to Galilee."

***

- "What did Rabbouni Ohannes mean, saying that you come after him but you have surpassed him because you were before him?"

I sat at the fire in the camp, eating breakfast together with some of Ohannes' disciples. I had been up on my feet for a week now, and was feeling stronger for each day. The one asking me was Andreas from Beth-Saida, a fisherman that had joined Ohannes several years earlier.

- "What does he say himself?" I asked back.

Andreas answered

- "He said before that you are the Messiah, come to free us and to build our new kingdom. But now he has started to talk about an inner kingdom of Allah's peace."

- "I have surpassed him because I have never left this Inner Kingdom", I said, "and I have been given the Mission from Allah to awaken everybody. Nobody has ever left The Kingdom of Allah, and to awaken to this truth is to be saved from suffering and death. So Allah has not asked me to be your Messiah. He has asked me to be your savior. Follow me and be a fisherman of lost souls, Andreas!"

Andreas stared at me, as if my words were incomprehensible to him. Then he slowly started to smile, and said

- "Master Yeshua, I know that master Ohannes believes that you and he share the same mission, and I know in my heart, hearing your words, that my mission now is to follow you. I will talk to master Ohannes about this and about my elder brother Shimon and our close friend Philippos, who is also from Beth-Saida. I want them to come and talk with you."

I hugged Andreas, and I kissed him, saying

- "Andreas, I have now selected my first disciple, and I am glad! We will leave for Galilee tomorrow, and I think many of you in Ohannes' camp will want to follow."

***

Andreas returned after an hour. He had talked with Ohannes, and he had then talked to his brother Shimon, who now had followed him back to me. We had been sitting around the fire, and Shimon was preparing a fish for food. Andreas had brought bread and dried meat. We ate together, and we talked the whole afternoon, as Andreas and Shimon had many questions.

As gentle and kind Andreas was, as harsh and inquisitive was his elder brother, and he posed many concrete questions on what kind of plans I had made.

At the same time, I felt that he had the same kind of fire within as I, and despite his suspiciousness, I felt more and more trust for this stern man.

- "Shimon", I said, "I asked your brother Andreas to follow me and to become a fisherman of souls. I would now like to ask you the same."

- "Yes", Shimon replied at once, "I will gladly. I am surprised by myself, because your answers to my questions have been hard to understand by my head, but my heart understands."

- "Shimon, my dear brother", I said, "I am glad. You are my second disciple. I will call you Shimon Petros, and on the rock you are, my new church will be built."

And I and Shimon, whom I now called Petros, continued to talk, while Andreas went away to fetch their friend Philippos. After a while he returned with him and with another of Ohannes' disciples, and when they were still at a distance, I heard the other disciple say

- "… can anything good come out of Nazareth?"

When they had sat down with us at the fire, I said

- "Welcome Philippos, and welcome Nethanel bar Talmai, the Israelite without deceit!"

The man I had called Nethanel stared at me and asked

- "How did you know my name, master?"

I said

- "I saw you under the fig tree just a moment ago. You sat there thinking of what you had heard of me, and you became surprised when Philippos came and asked you to follow, to talk to me about becoming my new disciples."

Both Nethanel and Philippos stared at me, and Nethanel exclaimed

- "Master, you are the Son of Allah!" and he knelt before me.

I laughed, raised him up and hugged him. Then I hugged Philippos, and I said

- "Yes I am, and so are you. When you realize this, you will be able to do what I do. But, welcome to my flock, my brothers. You are now the third and the fourth of my disciples."

The five of us sat the rest of the day and talked. Nethanel was unlike the others a scholar and came from a noble family originally from Geshur. His family now lived in Cana in Galilee. Nethanel had studied the scriptures for many years, and had many questions on my understandings of different topics.

Philippos was a fisherman like Andreas and Shimon, and had been with Ohannes longer than they. I felt that he had a warm heart but a pessimistic mind, and that one motive he had in following me was to avoid retributions on Ohannes from Herodes Antipas, even if his main motive still was a hunger for truth.

Before returning to our tents for the night, I told them that I planned to leave for Galilee the next day.

***

During the time next day, when I and Ohannes were busy gathering my things from his tent, many in his large group of followers came to talk with us, and many asked us if they could follow me instead of staying with Ohannes and follow him southwards.

Ohannes seemed relieved rather than disappointed, and from what he said during the day I understood that he had sometimes felt the responsibility for all the people in his camp as a burden – his group had grown to be as large as a village, almost two hundred men and women.

At the time for my departure, I had a group of more than seventy people that intended to follow me north.

Chapter 12. Aprilis 14 784.
Miryam Magdalene.

- "We have been traveling with you for five weeks now, Rabbouni Yeshua. Much has happened in this time."

We were sitting, Miryam from Magdala and I, in the inner court of the house of Jason bar Jacimus, where I and my twelve disciples lived, as honored guests of Jason. The rest of the group lived just outside Capernaum, in a tent camp besides the harbor, on the shore of the Sea of Galilee. Miryam had been somewhat of a leader of the group of the women already in Ohannes' group, a role she had retained in this group.

- "Yes it surely has", I agreed, "our voyage got a good start in Cana, at the wedding in the home of Nethanel's parents. That was really a contrast to our frugal household in Bethany."

- "Did you really turn water into wine there?" Miryam asked. "There has been much talk about that in the group."

- "No I didn't", I laughed, "but after the dinner I taught Jason and the Twelve the deep meditation of the East, and how to perceive beyond the illusion of the physical reality. Many of the Twelve have in a short time become quite skilled in getting to this inner state of the mind, and I think they together somehow managed to change Nethanel's reality, especially when he got to know that the wine delivery had failed to arrive."

- "Well, however this happened", Miryam said, "most of those I have heard talking about this are convinced that you performed a miracle, and they are taking this as a sign of your divine source."

I said
- "I do have a divine source. As do you and everybody else as well. The only difference between us is that I *know* this for a fact, while others may or may not believe it. There is a difference between believing and knowing. But, regarding miracles, this was not a miracle, it was magic."

- "Is that not the same thing?" Miryam asked, surprised.

- "No", I explained, "magic is something that changes the physical, in ways that seem not follow common sense. But it is still about the physical world and believing in magic still traps us in the kingdom of matter, possessions and the body. Sorcerers work with magic, miracle-workers with miracles."

- "And what then are miracles?"

- "Miracles are of the spirit", I said, "and a miracle is a profound change of the mind and in how one sees the world. To truly forgive an old enemy, and suddenly see him or her with new eyes, can be a miracle. Miracles always heal the soul, magic can imprison it, depending on what it is used for. Magic used as a tool for awakening *can* be good, but magic used to impress always imprisons. Miracles, like magic, can change the physical world and make changes to the body, but this is only something that follows naturally after the mind changes."

Miryam sat quiet a moment, in thoughts, and then said

- "I think I understand how you mean. But I do not think most of the Twelve see it this way. I think that those who are working men, like Shimon Petrus, Andreas, Philippos, Hakob the elder and Ohannes, they understand this, maybe not with their heads but in their hearts. The other ones believe more in what their heads are telling them, especially Nethanel and Te'oma the Essene, and also Matthias, Hakob the younger and Thaddeus. Shimon the zealot and Yehudah Iscariot, they believe only in the magic feats that they want you to perform as the coming king of the Jews, in throwing out the Romans."

- "I hear that you have gotten to know my Twelve quite well, Miryam", I smiled, "but I can understand that you do. I have seen them often sit and talk with you. It seems like your explanations of my teachings are easier to understand than when they come from me."

- "You have traveled the world", Miryam said carefully, searching for words, "and sometimes you use words and ideas that sound strange, and that defy common sense. I listen to you with my heart, and I do not interpret and compare with the scriptures, I just take it in and if it feels right, I can put my own words on it."

- "You are my thirteenth disciple and my most treasured one!" I said, smiling even broader.

- "Thank you master Yeshua", Miryam said, blushing, "but pray, do not say this in front of others. The Twelve will stop talking to me, and the women will spread rumors about you and me! Just sitting like this, alone with you in the house of Jason, even with servants around, gets me into enough trouble."

- "I understand, and I promise", I said, "but tell me, Miryam, what are your thoughts about how the Twelve became my disciples?"

Miryam sat silent again, recalling her memories from the weeks that had passed.

- "When we came to Beth-Saida word must have preceded us there, because I really became astonished when you talked to Hakob the elder and his brother Ohannes in the fishing harbor, and they decided to follow you even before talking to their father Zebedee. They must have heard about you before you came, and talked between themselves about following you. Admittingly, Zebedee is a wealthy man despite being a fisherman, and can afford many hired hands to do his work, but still... I don't want to speak badly about their mother Salome, but it was difficult not to laugh when she later at their home tried to make you grant her sons special titles in your coming kingdom", Miryam chuckled.

- "They *are* going to have special roles in the future, but not in the way she thinks", I said, "but how do you get along with Hakob and Ohannes themselves?"

- "I love them as were they my brothers. I know that they are going to follow you anywhere. But I think they sometimes should try to control their temper, especially Ohannes. I can see why you call them the Sons of Thunder."

- "Then, when we were back here in Capernaum", she continued, "I became astonished again, when you just walked up to Matthias at his tax collector's booth in the market, and after a few words from you, he just rose and followed us. This I would call a miracle, not that I hate tax collectors – I have never had much tax to pay – but I really see him differently now. And thanks to him, having that feast in his house in the evening the same day, his friends Hakob and Thaddeus also joined. Hakob the younger is the first tax collector I have met that seems to have a very strong moral on how to behave."

- "And Thaddeus, Hakob's younger brother, then", I ventured, "does his former alliance with the zealots scare you?"

- "Oh no, not at all", Miryam exclaimed, "I cannot understand how he could be in that group – that dear, tenderhearted, humble man. He is sometime a little childish even, I wonder if the Zealots did not make use of him because he trusts people so."

- "I love Yehudah as well", I said, "my Mission will need many of his kind… The remaining three then?"

I had come to know the Twelve well, but I also knew myself well, in that I see only peoples' souls. I therefore valued Miryam's powers of observation regarding peoples' personalities, which for me were in the background of what I perceived. And the fact remained, in the work we had ahead of us, both the souls and the personalities of the Twelve would matter.

- "Yehudah Te'oma, who you met at the gathering with your friends the Essenes, that is a sharp mind. I really admire how he questions you; he is the one that forces you to use words one can understand. And still when you do, he questions. Don't you feel badly when he does?"

- "No, not at all", I laughed, "as a matter of fact, I do not feel badly about what anyone does or says. I know that *everyone*, *whatever* he does, believes in his heart that it is the right thing to do. But their actions may come out of seeing the world, or a specific situation, in a mistaken way, and these actions may hurt others. But in the end, destructive actions always hurt oneself. In the East they call this Karma."

- "I remember you talking about this in Bethany across the Jordan", Miryam said, "but now I understand more how you mean. But still, don't you feel frustrated by his suspiciousness?"

- "No, I feel grateful", I answered, "because of him the understanding and learning of every one increases. His value for us cannot be overrated."

Miryam continued

- "Shimon the Canaanite and Yehuda Iscariot. These two are the only ones that can make me feel anxious sometimes. They feel like hard men, even if they have never said or done anything that has frightened me. I guess what influences me is knowing their background as rebels, and their pronounced harshness towards the Romans. It is also with these two I had had the most difficulties in trying to explain what you mean by the Kingdom of Allah. They seem to believe, almost as fanatics, in you becoming the new King of the Jews, here in Palestine."

- "Yes, I know", I said, and felt a bit tired at once. "But again, this is another example of how beliefs can bounce back. They will continue to believe this, and it will make them act in ways that will make them hurt themselves. But even so, everything that is going to happen is for the best."

Miryam looked at me, suddenly looking troubled. She asked

- "Do you have visions about what will happen to us, each one of us?"

I hesitated, knowing that this was a part of my reality that was the hardest for others to understand and to cope with. I said

- "Yes I do. But what will happen is not like following a marked pathway, and encountering different things, one after another. What will happen in the future is like a maze of different paths, and at each crossroad one will take one of the forks. Which one depends on both the choices oneself makes, and it may depend on choices and beliefs of others. So therefore, I very seldom want to talk with others about this. From my looking at the visions of the future, *my talking* about them is *one* of the different paths, and it is seldom a good one. If you *believe* that you know your future, you will without knowing it actually *create* this future.

In my case, I *never* make choices of my own, *except* the choice to follow what my Father tells me to do. *This* is my will, this is my choice, for this I am vigilant. He decides, *at my request*. Miryam, do you understand this?"

Miryam was quiet for a long time, then she sighed deeply and said

- "I think I understand. And I not only respect your choice, I truly believe that what you say and what you do is for the good of all of us, even for all mankind in the end. But", and now she chuckled a little, "as a woman, used to gossiping and making different theories about what others think, it can be very frustrating…"

I laughed, stood up and hugged Miryam warmly, and said

- "As I said, you are my most valued disciple, my dearest Miryam. I need your mind, your eyes and your ears, and foremost your heart. But let us now go to the camp, they have probably already prepared the evening meal, and I was to lead the large learning group tonight again."

And we went into the house to get Jason, as he had wished to participate in this day's meeting. Together the three of us walked through the narrow paths of Capernaum down to the harbor, where our camp was.

Chapter 13. December 30 784.
Rejection.

- "You have said it yourself, Yeshua", my brother Hakob said, "no prophet is welcome in his hometown."

I and Hakob sat in the inner court in our old home in Nazareth. The whole family had gathered here for my birthday; I had just turned thirty-one. Now only I and Hakob and our two sisters Esther and Rivka remained, our three other brothers Joses, Shimon and Yehudah had returned to their homes. It had been a fine reunion – I had not met my sisters for a long time, and both of them were now grownup, now twenty-two and twenty, married, with children of their own.

- "I have said so, but it still feels strange that they cannot see that I am a different person now", I said with a sigh.

- "It just confirms other things you have said", Hakob continued, "about how we create and see what we believe, not the opposite, that we believe when we see things be created."

- "Both of these opposites make me frustrated", I confessed. Besides my cousin Ohannes and Miryam Magdalene, my brother Hakob was one of the few persons I could be completely candid with. "The people here in the village cannot see past their inner image of young Yeshua, the son of Yosef the woodworker. And the people outside Nazareth cannot see past their inner image of the Messiah, and they remember miracles only as something *I* have performed, not realizing that miracles happen naturally when someone awakens."

- "I think your message is too radical. I think few realize that you are more radical than even the zealots", Hakob said. "And I do not think they understood you when you said 'The Spirit of the Lord is on me, because He has anointed me to proclaim good news to the poor'. For them this is the same as saying that you are their Messiah, with power to overthrow the Romans, and they can see with their own eyes that you do not have that power. No wonder they shouted and made you leave the synagogue."

- "What frustrates me is that they are right in seeing that I am not their Messiah, without seeing what I am!" I grumbled. "But do not misunderstand me, Hakob, I do not judge them for their beliefs. I am frustrated because I love them. These are my people, I have known them all my life, and I so wish they could accept my gift, the offer from my Father, to experience complete inner peace!"

Hakob sat silent for a long time, looking at me. Then he sighed, and said:

- "I think that as long as your *own* inner peace depends on whether people accept your gift or not, you are not free yourself. It might not be up to you to decide when a gift is truly received."

Hearing this from my brother, whom I loved and respected, whose support I needed and valued, made me suddenly angry, my heart started to pound and I clenched my fists, as if to lash out at him. Seeing this, he looked surprised and afraid, but he said nothing, he just continued to look at me.

At the same time, an inner part of me could observe myself, seeing my own anger, an emotion I had not thought I could harbor any longer. And I suddenly realized that I had harbored anger, but that I had repressed it to some deep recess in my soul. I closed my eyes and looked deeply within myself. I got an inner image of an angry teenage boy, frustrated at his father who does not listen and who does not even want to understand.

Sitting here, in my old home, I could suddenly feel the presence of Yosef, my father, and the presence of his angry son, Yeshua. And my heart filled with compassion for them both. I felt how my heart swelled of love, and it felt like a warm white light shone out from it. The light spread more and more, until we all three were enclosed in a large sphere of white light. A light of peace and forgiveness. I forgave my father Yosef completely, and I forgave myself.

I slowly opened my eyes, looked at Hakob, who still looked frightened and tense, and I said

- "Hakob, my dearest brother. You are completely right. Thank you."

I stood up, and he did as well, looking bewildered. I went to him and I embraced him and I kissed him on both of his cheeks. We stood, embracing each other for a long time. When we sat down again, I could see tears in his eyes, but he looked relieved, even peaceful.

***

Later the same day, Hakob and I sat again in the inner court. Our mother Miryam and our sisters were cleaning away the table in the front room after the midday meal.

We had talked about anger and frustration, how there is really no difference between hate and mere irritation, as both are equally strong obstacles to forgiveness and inner peace.

- "Was it the same thing that happened with you last Passover, when you threw out the moneylenders from the Temple?" Hakob asked.

- "Yes and no", I said. "I have actually thought about that today, after our talk this morning. I think it was both. Part of it was my frustration from people not wanting to understand. Another part was something I learnt in Muktinath. Sometimes, when a lama is guiding a disciple that has come very far, and the disciple is struggling with the last remnants of attachment to earthly needs, awakening can happen by exposing the disciple to a sudden shock, like a blow over the head, or by letting something completely unexpected happen."

- "So you planned it to happen?" Hakob asked.

- "I could have done that", I said, "and it would have been better if I had done so. As it was now, I had actually been thinking of the lama's teaching, but my anger came before my brain."

- "Well, in any case, what you did has spread all around the country, that's for sure", Hakob said with a smile. "Both how you could do that because you are the true Messiah, and others that say it just proves the falsity of your message of peace."

- "Yes, I know", I sighed, "but maybe something good will come out of it. At least people will maybe be able to see that I am a human being just as everyone else, and then also take in that I am a human being that has awoken to the True World, the Kingdom of Allah. And that this is what I wish for everyone."

- "Talking about stories about you that spread, I think your awakening of even a few will make people believe in your message", Hakob said. "Many have come to you to be baptized by you and the Twelve, and there are now even believers in Samaria, after you told that woman in Sychar about her previous life."

- "Yes", I agreed, "*believing* in that it is *possible* to awaken, believing in that miracles are possible, will in itself make it more possible. I remember how I a long time ago said to my friend in Muktinath, the lama Devapala, that teaching is like spreading seeds, where some end up on barren rock, others in the weed and are smothered, and some again in fertile soil."

Hakob sat quiet, I could see he was searching for words. Finally, he said

- "There have been rumors about miracles. You have healed a few, people suffering from life-long sickness…"

- "Yes, healing has happened", I said, "and this is another example of how hard it obviously is to understand my message. In these cases, my words and my touch, and my complete acceptance of them as sinless human beings, made their eyes open and they could suddenly see themselves, as the divine beings they are, blessed by Allah. And seeing, they healed themselves. But even when I said so to them, they still fell back to their old way of regarding themselves, and told everyone around than *I* had healed them, that *I* had performed the miracle."

- "But that being so cannot stop you from seeing them as they truly are, can it?" Hakob said. "Is this not another good example of a gift where you do not know when it is going to be truly received?"

Hearing this for the second time this day now just made me feel amused by myself, and thankful for my brother's gentle reminder, and I smiled:

- "Nothing will stop me from seeing by brothers and sisters as Allah's children. I sow seeds, and it is up to my Father to make them take root and to grow.

Hakob, my brother, will you join with me in a prayer I have taught my disciples?"

He agreed, we both closed our eyes, and I recited:

- "Our Father who art in heaven.
Hallowed be thy Name.
Thy Kingdom is here.
Thy will be done,
on earth as in heaven.
Give us what we truly need
and forgive us our mistaken thoughts,
for us to forgive others for theirs.
Help us see temptation,
so that we avoid doing evil.
Ours is the Kingdom,
and the power, and the glory,
for ever and ever.
Amen."

Chapter 14. Quintilis 14 785.
The Sermon on the Mount.

The time that had passed since my visit in Nazareth had been a time of intense teaching and meeting with larger and larger groups of people. From our now quite permanent camp in Capernaum, we had made long journeys around Galilee. We had also been down once to Jerusalem for Passover.

More and more miracles of healing happened, as more people started to believe the possibility of healing, although none were able to take the step to belief in self-healing, despite my constant reminders 'Your faith has healed you'. But my beloved brother Hakob's reminder helped me to remember to let this be, and to put my own faith in my Father's hands.

This day, the summer heat had abated some. Many had asked my disciples to meet with me, and Petros had decided for a larger meeting than usual, where I would spend a whole day teaching. The disciples had told people to meet us at Mount Eremos, a couple of hours' walk northeast from Capernaum.

When we came there in the morning, many hundred had already gathered, and many in our group had to spend the first hour to arrange how people should sit in order for all to hear.

With assistance from local woodworkers, a platform had been erected, with a plank wall behind to make my voice heard downwards into the valley below. I sat on a stool on the platform and the Twelve were seated on a low bench behind me, where they could lean against the planking behind.

The weather was perfect for an occasion like this, a little cloudy and with no wind at all. As I sat, looking over the crowds, I could hear some talking with low voices with each other, but most of the people present were just looking at us, and it was almost completely quiet.

As this was a larger gathering than usual, we had not planned to have any special breaks for questions and discussions, as we in most cases else had in our smaller gatherings. For this day I had planned a longer teaching, with time for questions afterwards in smaller groups. As soon as I started to speak, the crowd of people, that now had grown to almost a thousand, became completely silent.

- "First, beloved brothers and sisters, I will tell you the ten ways by which you can be blessed. These, and more, are the teachings I have given my twelve disciples here on the stage behind me, and to all the ones that have followed us.

> Blessed are those not imprisoning with thoughts,
> for theirs is the kingdom in heaven.

> Blessed are those who mourn,
> they will be comforted.

> Blessed are the humble,
> they will inherit the earth.
>
> Blessed are those who hunger for Truth,
> they will find it.
>
> Blessed are those who forgive,
> they will be forgiven.
>
> Blessed are those who see with love,
> they will see Allah.
>
> Blessed are the miracle-workers,
> they will be called children of Allah.
>
> Blessed are those persecuted for talking of Truth,
> theirs is the Kingdom of Heaven.

And these ways are not the only ones. There are many paths that lead to our Father, and you can choose any of them.

Blessed are you even when you are insulted, persecuted or becoming victim of false accusations because of listening to me and doing my work. Rejoice and be glad, because your reward will be great.

You who spread my word are the salt of the earth. But if the salt loses its saltiness, how can it be made salty again? It is no longer good for anything, except to be thrown out and trampled underfoot.

You who spread my word are the light of the world. A town built on a hill cannot be hidden. Neither do people light a lamp and put it under a bowl. Instead they put it on its stand, and it gives light to everyone in the house. In the same way, let your light shine before others, that they may see your good deeds and glorify our Father in heaven."

An old man, bald and with a large white beard, stood up and asked

- "But, master, if someone has sinned he has to atone and make sacrifices to be worthy of blessing again. What do you say about sin?"

I answered him

- "You have heard that it was said to the people long ago, 'You shall not murder. Anyone who murders will be subject to judgment.'

But I tell you that anyone who is angry with a brother or sister will in reality be judging himself. Again, anyone who says to a brother or sister, 'Raca' is imprisoning himself by guilt. And anyone who says, 'You fool!' will be in danger of creating hell for oneself.

Therefore, if you are offering your gift at the altar and there remember that your brother or sister has something against you, leave your gift there in front of the altar. First go and be reconciled to them; then come and offer your gift.

Settle matters quickly with your adversary who is taking you to court. Do it while you are still together on the way, or your adversary may hand you over to the judge, and the judge may hand you over to the officer, and you may be thrown into prison. Truly I tell you, you will not get out until you have paid the last penny. And the prison is of your own making."

The old man had remained standing, and he said

- "How can you compare being angry with murder?"

I said

- "There is no sin, there is only wrong-mindedness. The wrong-minded see the world as hostile and they think they have to do what they do to protect themselves. Sometimes this leads to great mistakes. Both the one who says 'Raca' to his brother, and the one wanting to kill need to forgive. Sometimes they first need to be forgiven before they can forgive themselves, to be able to become right-minded."

- "So you forgive the murderer and let the crime pass?" the old man exclaimed angrily.

- "You shall forgive and you shall act. But the purpose of your action shall be to help him become right-minded, and the most loving thing you can do then to protect him from killing again is locking him up, and then patiently try to wake him up to right-mindedness."

- "But surely, every sensible person knows that the murderer deserves to be executed!"

- "You cannot help anybody become right-minded by being wrong-minded yourself" I said. "To execute is to murder."

The old man sat down, looking both bewildered and angry, shaking his head. A young man behind him now stood up and asked

- "So you say that we shall protect people from acting on their mistaken thoughts. I can understand that the murderer may have become blinded by anger, but how can you say that about adultery? Those surely deserve to be stoned!"

I answered

- "You have heard that it was said, 'You shall not commit adultery.'

But I tell you that anyone who looks at another person as something to possess has already become trapped in illusion, believing that true happiness comes only from meeting the needs of your body. Love each other, give pleasure to each other, but use your relationship as a path to Allah, by regarding each other as divine souls that cannot be owned. If a part of your mind causes you to stumble, gouge it out and throw it away. It is better to lose one part of your mind than for your whole soul to go into hell.

The mistake done is not the adultery itself, it is the dishonesty. Forgive yourself that you devotion to your wife or your husband may not last a lifetime, and be honest. This honesty may lead to divorce.

It has been said, 'Anyone who divorces his wife must give her a certificate of divorce.'

All relationships can be made holy, if they are used for giving out Allah's love to another. But even holy relationships may not be meant to last forever, so I tell you, give not only a certificate of divorce; settle all things justly and with honesty, so that you can walk away on your different paths as friends."

The young man cried indignantly

- "But surely, the adulterer has broken his or her oath! That is an oath to Allah!"

I smiled at him and said

- "You have heard that it was said, 'Do not break your oath, but fulfill to the Lord the vows you have sworn.'

But I tell you, do not swear an oath at all: either to Allah, or to earthly powers, or to your honor, because you cannot change your thoughts. All you need to say is simply 'Yes' or 'No'; anything beyond this comes from a part of your mind that is not honest."

Now many started to talk among themselves, and a man clad in a long mantle stood up and said

- "A man whose wife has been with another man is entitled to revenge. A man whose son has been murdered is entitled to revenge. Why should he forgive?"

I had heard these arguments so many times that I felt weary. But, I closed my eyes and let my impatience pass, looked at him and said

- "You have heard that it was said, 'Eye for eye, and tooth for tooth.'

But I tell you, do not resist a person who seeks to be evil. If anyone slaps you on the right cheek, turn to them the other cheek also. And if anyone wants to sue you and take your shirt, hand over your coat as well. If anyone forces you to go one mile, go with them two miles. Give to the one who asks you, and do not turn away from the one who wants to borrow from you. Forgive and you will be forgiven.

You have heard that it was said, 'Love your neighbor and hate your enemy.'

But I tell you, love your enemies and pray for those who persecute you, that you may be children of your Father in heaven. He causes his sun to rise on the evil and the good, and sends rain on the righteous and the unrighteous. If you love those who love you, what reward will you get? Are not even the tax collectors doing that? And if you greet only your own people, what are you doing more than others? Do not even pagans do that? Be generous and forgiving, therefore, as your heavenly Father forgives all and offers us everything."

At this many stood up and came nearer the platform. They gathered around, agitated, many raised their voices, trying to be heard. The old man with the white beard made his way through the crowd, came up and slammed his walking staff into the platform, and the sound of this silenced the others. He said

- "This is not what a righteous man can do! To defend one's honor is Allah's will! We give to the poor and we remember our prayers and we follow the commandments. That should be enough!"

Everyone looked at me, some were smiling triumphantly at this irrefutable statement. I smiled gently at them, held my arms out and said

- "Do you want to be righteous or do you want to happy? To be righteous, giving in order to be honored by others, is not the same as doing the right thing. The right thing is to give from your heart, without any sacrifice, because to give truly is to receive. Give and you will be given. Give all and you will be given all.

When you pray, do not be like the hypocrites, for they love to pray standing in the synagogues and on the street corners to be seen by others. When you pray, go into your room, close the door and pray to your Father, who is unseen. Then your Father, who sees what is done in secret, will give you what you need. And when you pray, do not keep on babbling like the pious scripture-followers, for they think they will be heard because of their many words. You need not be like them, for your Father knows what you need before you ask him.

This, then, is how you can pray:

Our Father who art in heaven.
Hallowed be thy Name.
Thy Kingdom is here.
Thy will be done, on earth as in heaven.
Give us what we truly need and forgive us our mistaken thoughts,
for us to forgive others for theirs.
Help us see temptation, so that we avoid doing evil.
Ours is the Kingdom, and the power, and the glory, for ever and ever.
Amen.

For if you forgive other people when they sin against you, you will realize that your heavenly Father has already forgiven. But if you do not forgive others their sins, you will not be able to forgive yourself and you will never know your Father's forgiveness."

At this all who stood near the platform returned to where they had been sitting before. Many shook their heads but they did not say anything more.

A man in fine clothes stood up. He was sitting among women and children, which seemed to be his family. He said

- "Your disciples have left everything when they followed you. When you say that we shall not pray for more than we need, how shall I be able to provide for my large family?"

I heard this man being torn between his need for feeling secure and his longing for being worthy in Allah's eyes, and I felt compassion for him. I said

- "Do not store up for yourself treasures on earth, where moths and vermin destroy, and where thieves break in and steal. But store up for yourself treasures in heaven, where moths and vermin do not destroy, and where thieves do not break in and steal. For where your treasure is, there your heart will be also.

The eye is the lamp of the body. If your eyes are healthy, your whole body will be full of light. But if your eyes are unhealthy, your whole body will be full of darkness. If then the light within you is darkness, how great is that darkness!

No one can serve two masters. Either you will hate the one and love the other, or you will be devoted to the one and despise the other. You cannot serve both Allah and Mammon.

Therefore I tell you, do not worry about your life, what you will eat or drink; or about your body, what you will wear. Is not life more than food, and the body more than clothes? Can any one of you by worrying add a single hour to your life?

And why do you worry about clothes? See how the flowers of the field grow. They do not labor or spin. Yet I tell you that not even Solomon in all his splendor was dressed like one of these. So do not worry, saying, 'What shall we eat?' or 'What shall we drink?' or 'What shall we wear?' The greedy run after all these things, imprisoning themselves in these thoughts. Seek first your Father's kingdom and his Truth, and all these things will be given to you as well. Therefore do not worry about tomorrow, for tomorrow will worry about itself. Each day has enough trouble of its own."

- "So the ones that serve Mammon and gather riches for themselves, are they judged unworthy by Allah?" a young man asked.

To this I answered

- "Allah does not judge, He loves each one of you regardless of what you do. But He weeps for those of you who make yourselves deaf and blind against His love. Heal your deafness and your blindness by forgiving your brothers and your sisters. Do not judge, or you will judge yourself. For in the same way you judge others, you will be judged by yourself, and with the measure you use, it will be measured to you.

Why do you look at the speck of sawdust in your brother's eye and pay no attention to the plank in your own eye? How can you say to your brother, 'Let me take the speck out of your eye', when all the time there is a plank in your own eye? You hypocrite, first take the plank out of your own eye, and then you will see clearly to remove the speck from your brother's eye.

So what can be said about what you need to do, for finding Allah?

Ask and it will be given to you; seek and you will find; knock and the door will be opened to you. For everyone who asks receives; the one who seeks finds; and to the one who knocks, the door will be opened.

Which of you, if your son asks for bread, will give him a stone? Or if he asks for a fish, will give him a snake? If you, then, though you have mistaken thoughts, know how to give good gifts to your children, how much more will your Father in heaven give good gifts to those who ask him!

So this is my Golden Rule: In everything, do to others what you would have them do to you.

This sums up the real truth of the Law and the Prophets.

Enter through the narrow gate. For wide is the gate and broad is the road that leads to destruction, and many enter through it. But tight is the gate and narrow is the road that leads to Life and only a few find it."

- "Master", the young man continued, "you talk like a prophet yourself, and you are not even a rabbi. How can we know that what you say is true? How can we know that those claiming to speak your message are saying the same thing as you do?"

I nodded at him and said

- "Yes, there are false prophets, and you need to be watchful. They come to you in sheep's clothing, but inwardly they are ferocious wolves. But, by their fruit you will recognize them. Do people pick grapes from thornbushes, or figs from thistles? Likewise, every good tree bears good fruit, but a bad tree bears bad fruit. A good tree cannot bear bad fruit, and a bad tree cannot bear good fruit. Forgive them for the bad fruit, but do not eat it. Love them and their thoughts will heal.

And yes, there can come false disciples. Not everyone who says to me, 'Lord, Lord,' will because of this enter the kingdom of heaven, this will the one who does the will of my Father who is in heaven. Many will say to me on that day, 'Lord, Lord, did we not prophesy in your name and in your name drive out demons and in your name perform many miracles?'

Then I will tell them plainly, 'You have not learnt who you really are. You are still imprisoning yourself in hell.' And I will feel pity for them, but they will have merely wasted their time, nothing more. The only thing needed to become my true disciple is honesty and a little willingness.

So, dear brothers and sisters, this is what I finally want to tell you today:

Everyone who hears these words of mine and puts them into practice is like a wise man who built his house on the rock. The rain came down, the streams rose, and the winds blew and beat against that house; yet it did not fall, because it had its foundation on the rock.

But everyone who hears these words of mine and does not put them into practice is like a foolish man who built his house on sand. The rain came down, the streams rose, and the winds blew and beat against that house, and it fell with a great crash."

***

With this I had ended my teaching. I and the Twelve stood up and went down to the crowd. Separately, we walked around the rest of the day, stopping at each person wanting to talk or that had a question. Many had brought food and water and invited us to share their meal, and both I and the ones among the Twelve now and then sat down with the ones offering their food.

Many were still angry, and questioned me much, especially about what I had said about revenge and enemies, which they felt went against all common sense. Many asked me more about adultery and divorce, and were angry because they believed I had spoken against the Law.

But many were curious and wanted to hear more. Many were awed, asking how I could speak with such authority about things like sin and forgiveness, despite not being a priest. Many asked how they could become followers, and these I sent to the Twelve to make arrangements.

***

When we were on our way back to Capernaum, we were met by friends to the centurion of the area. He had sent them to me because his most valued servant had become ill and was dying, and he had heard of my powers to heal. The friends had a message from the centurion, which said

- "Lord, I do not deserve to have you come under my roof. But say the word, and my servant will be healed. For I myself am also a man under authority, with soldiers under me. I tell this one, 'Go', and he goes; and that one, 'Come', and he comes. I say to my servant, 'Do this', and he does it."

I said to his friends

- "I am amazed, I have not found such great faith even in Israel. But go tell your friend that with his authority he can make his servant heal himself. He needs only see his servant as a divine child of Allah, having a soul free of sickness and invulnerable to death, and the body will obey and will heal."

***

Late in the evening the same day, a messenger came to Jason's house to report that the centurion's servant miraculously had recovered, and that the centurion had asked if there was anything in our camp his servants or his soldiers could help us with.

And for the rest of the time we were in Capernaum, and also when we came back from our tours in the country, the centurion always offered his help.

Chapter 15. Sextilis 5 785.
The Emissaries.

- "But we cannot do this without you, master", Petros exclaimed, "People expect so much now, they are hungering for your words and your healing, and they will become angry if they see us coming by ourselves."

We sat in the inner court of Jason's house, I together with the Twelve, and we had just shared breakfast.

I smiled and said

- "Petros, my dear brother. I think I have more faith in you than you have yourself. My words you know by now, and you can now have your own words say the same. As for my powers of healing, we have talked about this at length, and maybe we need to talk more about this before I send you twelve out in Galilee by yourselves, two and two of you on your own path."

- "We have healed people, master, but never without you being near", Ohannes said, "how can we know we have your powers, just because you say we have?"

- "Tell me, Ohannes", I said, "can you forgive the blind man for believing he cannot see?"

- "Of course, master!" Ohannes answered, looking surprised. "It is not his fault, he didn't chose to become blind."

- "But now tell me", I continued, "can you forgive the lecherous man that commits adultery with young women?"

Ohannes sat without speaking for a moment, reflecting on these two examples, and finally said

- "I know you have said that the lecherous man believes he *has* to do what he does to gain happiness in his life, and that we should forgive him, but still..."

- "There are but *two* things people feel, deep in their hearts", I said. "Love or fear. The lecherous man, even if he believes he gives love and receives love, from many sources, he is driven by fear. By extending your love and your forgiveness to him he may awaken from his nightmare and discover that his fear is completely unnecessary."

- "I have come to understand", now said Hakob the younger, "that my eyes are clouded. If I could be vigilant for my Father and for His way of seeing us, I would always be able to see that fear. And seeing it, my natural reaction *would* be to forgive."

I nodded to Hakob and said, looking around at all sitting on stools in a circle around me

- "If you cannot see your brother with clear eyes, your mind will make up an inner image of him, an image of how you value him and how you judge him. This image may make it impossible for you to forgive.

But if you see him with clear eyes, seeing who he *really* is behind his fears and his destructive behavior, seeing the true person behind all the veils he has put in front of him, to protect himself, then *you cannot do anything else* than forgive and to love him."

- "But, what has this to do with healing?" Ohannes asked.

- "This is what healing is about", I said, "When you are fully able to see the lecherous man with the same compassion as you feel for the poor blind man, then you will be able to heal the blind man's damaged eyesight."

- "So you mean that the compassion I feel for the blind man is not enough", Petros said, "it is not until I can feel this compassion for *anyone* that I can heal the blind man?"

- "You are on the right track", I said, "but again, it will not be you who heal. By seeing the blind man in this way, but not valuing him any different from how you value anyone else, disregarding their so called sins, the blind man will be able to see himself in the same way, and his mind will heal. And when the mind heals, the body just follows."

- "But master", Yehudah Te'oma angrily retorted, "are you saying that the body does not have a will of its own? We all know how things can make the body sick, how violence from others can wound it."

- "Yehudah, I love your scrutinizing mind", I said. Partly you are right. We are seldom prepared when things happen to us, and the body reacts. But if we make our body to be our only reality, it will control the mind. The mind in itself is invulnerable and eternal, and as soon as we know this, we know that it is the mind which controls the body. By seeing oneself invulnerable, the body will then just follow this, and it will heal itself."

- "Tell that to a man hanging on the cross", Yehudah muttered, obviously not convinced, "that his mind is unharmed and that he will survive."

- "That is an extreme example", I said, "and every child has to learn to crawl before learning to walk. But I say to you truly, there will come a day when I will say that to a man hanging on the cross."

Yehudah Te'oma shook his head but did not say anything more about this.

- "This will not be the last time we talk about this, because this is our mission. We are going to awaken mankind; we are going awaken each man and woman on the Earth. But this awakening has to be preceded by healing, and with healing I mean a healing of the mind.

But, let us talk of what you have ahead. I am sending you out like sheep among wolves. Therefore be as shrewd as snakes and as innocent as doves. Be on your guard; you will be handed over to the local councils and be flogged in the synagogues. On my account you will be brought before governors and kings as witnesses to them and to the Gentiles.

But when they arrest you, do not worry about what to say or how to say it. At that time you will be given what to say, for it will not be you speaking, but the Holy Spirit of your Father speaking through you.

So do not be afraid of them, for there is nothing concealed that will not be disclosed, or hidden that will not be made known. What I tell you in the dark, speak in the daylight; what is whispered in your ear, proclaim from the roofs. Do not be afraid of those who kill the body but cannot kill the soul."

- "Thank you master Yeshua", said Nethanel, "for your trust in us. I for one feel now that I really want to do what my Father will tell me to do. I know in my heart that you are His messenger, but how will I know my Father's will when I am out there all by myself?"

- "If you do not think about it", I said, "your Father's words will be the ones you say. But if you *do* think of it, you may raise an obstacle against hearing His words, and you may replace them with your own. But then, the *only* thing you need to do is to think 'What would master Yeshua had said or done now', and I will be there in spirit for you, and the words of the Father will flow through you."

- "I believe they will", Nethanel said slowly, "I actually believe they will..."

We spent many more hours talking, most of the time about the practical details of their different paths. Which villages and towns each pair of the disciples would visit, how to find people to stay with, which of the followers in our larger group that would accompany them. Yehudah Iscariot, having good skills in organizing acquired in his former life in rebel groups as an assassin, was given the task of organizing our "raids" around the country.

When I went to bed that evening, I felt complete trust in my 'Emissaries' that I was about to send out in the world, to spread my word.

From my inner visions I knew that the period to come would not be the last for these twelve men in following our mission. They would do this for the rest of their physical lives, and many would return to Earth many times to fulfil their tasks.

The rolling stone had been set in motion, and never would moss grow on it …

Chapter 16. Ianuarius 15 786.
Ohannes' death.

- "Not even talking about Ohannes the Baptist in the synagogue could make them listen to me", I complained to Hakob, my brother. "One would think that his cruel death in prison should have moved them."

It was late evening. He and I sat in the front room of our old home; our mother had already retired for the night in the inner room.

- "Their inner image of who they think you are goes deep", Hakob said, "and you are probably never going to be able to change that. But I am happy that mother and all of us see your true self, even if we do not call you master, Yeshua. I remember how we in the beginning thought that you had become possessed, and we wanted to bring you home with us. But what will you do now? Many of Ohannes' followers have been in your group for a long time."

- "Yes, they have", I said, "and it feels heavy to meet their grief, on top of my own. I should have known that he had been captured, I should have done something…"

- "I know you, Yeshua", Hakob said, "and I am the one that has known about your visions of the future the longest time of all. I know how they first felt like a gift, but how they more and more have become a burden for you. I can really understand how you have needed to limit your visions, and to stay in the now, in all that you and your group have been doing in so many places."

- "I warned Ohannes against judging, and now he even brought Herodes Antipas' wrath over him…" I said. "I could have warned him about this."

- "Listen, Yeshua, you are my older brother, and I truly believe you are enlightened", Hakob said impatiently, and took my hands in his, "but in this case I must remind you of your own sayings about the free will and about the crossroads we encounter. And I also feel I have to remind you, who talk so often about forgiveness, to remember to forgive yourself. Maybe you think of yourself as divine, but Yeshua, you *are* not Allah, you are human!"

Shaken by his words, I remained silent for a long time. Then I smiled, squeezed his hands, and said

- "Thank you again, Hakob, my dearest brother. Allah has given a large gift to me being your brother. You are right, as before. What you dare to say to me none else would dare. And you are right, I am human. Ohannes' death grieves me, and just now it feels like all the enlightened words I spread to others do not help me."

- "So, if you would allow yourself to be just human for once", Hakob said, "what would you do then? It seems to me that the mission you have laid on yourself and on your follower sometimes requires an inhuman effort."

His words made me relax, and I leaned back, closing my eyes. Not to go into an inner vision this time, but just to relax, to let myself just feel what I felt. And after a while I opened my eyes and said

- "I will go back to Beth-Saida and rest. I think we all need rest, and many of us need to grieve, and grief can never be hurried. It can be repressed, it can be rationalized, but it does not disappear by doing that. Grief is a wound that needs healing, and this healing is different from the body's. The body can heal in an instant, but grief demands time, and this time not even I can alter."

- "I see you as a wise man, Yeshua, and I have often heard you pronounce very wise things", Hakob said, smiling, "but this I think is the wisest thing I have heard from you in a long time."

In our grief, and I know Hakob grieved Ohannes as much as I, we laughed and hugged each other.

***

And as I said I would, I together with the Twelve and together with all of the others in our group, traveled to Beth-Saida, where we stayed for four months. The group lived in a tent camp outside the village, I and the twelve stayed in Zebedee's house, father of Hakob the elder and Ohannes.

I rested from preaching, rested from confronting priests and the Pharisees, and rested from all the discussions with the masses of people demanding to be saved from Roman oppression. I allowed myself to rest, to discuss and teach together with just the Twelve and with Miryam.

I allowed myself to fully human, and I realized that this period was as important to my mission as everything else we had done. If I did not let myself be human, with human weaknesses and needs, how would I ever understand others fully?

Chapter 17. Aprilis 18 786.
Walking on water.

We had, after the period when we had withdrawn to Beth-Saida, had our first meeting with people, on the hills east of Gergesa on the eastern shore of the Sea of Galilee. I had preached to a large crowd and we had later walked around, talking with people for many hours. Many had awakened and healed themselves from different ailments.

Used to the calm life we had enjoyed in Beth-Saida, I felt wary, so when the Twelve said that we had to hurry on to Genesareth, I told them I needed to go up on the mountain and meditate, and that I would follow our larger group, which would start to walk north of the lake next morning.

They still wanted to leave immediately by themselves, to prepare the next meeting in Genesareth, and they had borrowed a boat, with which they would sail over the lake, saving effort and time.

We left each other; they hurried down to the harbor, and I walked by myself up the hill. It felt good to be completely alone for once.

I reached a high point in the hills, found a peaceful spot under a tree, sat down in the shade, and started to meditate. I had had the habit of meditating each morning and each evening for many years now, and I quickly entered a deep state of tranquility, which due to the fact that I was completely alone, became deeper than usual.

In contrast to my usual meditations, I this time got a vivid inner vision, and this was the first time it was not of the future, it was present time. In my vision, I was out in the middle of the Sea of Galilee, standing in the air just above the water. I saw the boat with my twelve disciples not far from where I was, at a distance of around twenty cubits, and a sudden storm had blown up. They had managed to lower their sails, and were trying to keep the bow against the gale and the waves, that had grown high. I saw how some of them were frantically pouring out water from the boat with buckets.

They stared and pointed at me, and I could hear Petros shout something.

Suddenly I was in the boat, sitting on the aft bench besides Petros, who held the tiller. I now realized that this was no vision, and as it was when I discovered my ability for prescience when I was a child: I realized that this ability, to be anywhere just by visualizing it clearly, was an ability I had had always, but that it had been outside my awareness. I willed time to stop, and the waves froze, looking like mountains of green glass, and it became completely quiet.

I said

- "It is really I. Do not be afraid."

Petros, who had looked completely paralyzed, as all the others, now let go of the tiller, and grabbed my left arm, and said

- "Master Yeshua. It is you. We thought our last moment had come, and that it was a ghost, coming from the kingdom of death! But what is happening, what are you doing? How did you still the storm?"

I laughed and said

- "You have heard me talk of the power of the mind. How we create what we believe. I have come here to give you an experience of this power. I have taught you how to stop the flow of time in meditation, and now I show you how you can stop the flow of time also in full awareness. The storm is still going on, but not in this instant. This instant, just now, is all there is."

- "But you walked on the water!" Thaddeus exclaimed.

- "I did not really", I said, "I merely willed to be at that point in space. Anyone of you can do the same."

- "My senses tell me that you are showing me something my brain cannot comprehend, but which I know is true", said Petros. "Show me how to do that!"

- "Take my hand", I said to him. He took me by my hand, and I willed us to be where I had been before, twenty cubits from the boat. It felt like we were standing on rock. Shimon Petros stared at the others over in the boat, and he laughed happily, as an infant who has just learnt to stand up by himself for the very first time.

Then he looked down, saw the shimmering green surface of the water, yelped and started to sink down, and clutched both his hands around my arm. I laughed and pulled him up, and said

- "Shimon Petros, where is your faith? Just see it as solid ground!"

He closed his eyes, sighed with relief, opened them again, and now remained standing. Together, we walked on the surface of the lake over to the others, and climbed aboard the boat.

Everybody were struck dumb by seeing this. Nethanel was the first to find his words again:

- "Master Yeshua. This must prove, beyond any doubt, that you are Allah's Son, the Messiah."

- "No, as I had said to you again and again", I said, "this proves that we all create the reality we experience. It may also prove that my power of *persuasion* is greater than anyone else's, but this proves the powers of the mind, both my mind and yours. And what we have created together with our minds here on Earth is the opposite of the Kingdom of Allah. Where the truth is that we cannot die, we have invented death. Where the truth is that there is only love, we have invented hell."

- "But in now teaching us this, we can do anything!" Yehudah Te'oma said.

- "Again, no, not yet", I said, "this is but the first tiny step. With the help of my persuasion, you have stopped the flow of time. But you are still not in the Kingdom of Allah. To complete this learning, you will have to choose the one reality before the other, in everything that will happen. To experience Allah's Love, extend love and forgiveness. As soon as you use the power of the mind for anything else, or performing miracles in order to impress, you will be trapped again in the world you have made up."

- "But how shall we ever learn?" Ohannes said. "We do not have the powers that you have."

- "The powers I have demonstrated are not my own. As soon as you rely on your own powers you are trapped again. The only thing Allah needs, to extend his power to you, is but a little willingness from your side. And persistence of course, even vigilance. What has happened here today will help you to have faith in Him.

But now, my dear brothers, we need to go on, we have others to teach, we have a world to save! The wind will turn, so set sails, and let us rush to Genesareth!"

And at this instant, the gale continued, the boat rocked wildly, and all the men shouted, terrified. But Petros steered the boat, his knuckles white with strain, the ones holding the buckets started to empty the boat again from water, as it reached almost to our knees. And after a moment the wind turned, and Petros could steer the boat with the wind. Hakob the elder and his brother set the foresail, and the boat raced ahead westward with the waves.

***

A couple of days later, the rest of our group arrived, and busied themselves in setting up camp and preparing for the next meeting.

As some had seen me walk away from the Twelve in Gergesa, and had seen them sail away without me, there were many questions on how I had arrived here before them. The Twelve had tried to convey their experience on the lake to the others, but few could comprehend what they tried to describe, and many different stories about my ability to walk on water arose and were later spread to many.

I felt frustrated by this. As with many others myths about me, it became another obstacle against really listening to my message.

But I reminded myself often of my brother Hakob's wise words, *"As long as your own inner peace depends on whether people accept your gift or not, you are not free yourself. It might not be up to you to decide when a gift is truly received."*

Chapter 18. Quintilis 20 786.
Preparation.

The heat of the summer had started to abate, and I and the Twelve were sitting inside a pagan temple, The Gates of Hades, near the town of Caesarea Philippi.

- "We can see that you are wary again, master", Ohannes said. "This is the fourth time we withdraw from people this year."

- "Yes, my brothers", I admitted, "I am wary. But we have done many things, and many have awoken to their true selves, healing themselves. During our long trip up north to Tyros and Sidon we have sown many seeds among the gentiles. I hope this will convince people in Galilee that I am not merely the savior of Israel's lost sheep, but a herdsman looking for every lost sheep in the entire world."

- "You did not convince the Pharisees and the Sadducees down at Dalmanutha." Matthias chuckled, "Asking you for signs made it obvious they still think that you claim being the Messiah. You made them upset, talking about the signs of coming weather, and saying that the signs are here for anyone to see."

- "The fact they were testing me is a sign in itself. It is a sign of an inner struggle against seeds having taken root in their stubborn souls as well", I said, "and I feel compassion for them – such faith! If they could only put their faith in Truth instead of in what they have made up. But they are my lost sheep as well."

- "Pharisees and Sadducees! They are not lost sheep, they are collaborating with the Romans, using the Law to enslave us. They are evil!" Andreas said angrily.

- "Andreas, my dear brother. Now your temper is blowing your senses away again", I smiled, "remember there are no evil people. But there are many that harbor terror for Allah's wrath behind their righteous and proud faces. And fearful people can be dangerous. The only way to convince them is to show them that what they fear does not exist."

- "But how are we ever going to be able to do this?" Yehudah Te'oma asked. "They will never listen!"

- "I will make them listen, by showing them a sign than no one will be able to deny", I said. "And this will happen in less than a year from today, and it will be my final teaching in the human life I have lived together with you here on Earth. I will let myself be killed by these fearful people, and then I will come back and show myself a final time in the physical form I have now, and after that I will exist in spirit, for anyone to listen to and to learn from."

All twelve stared at me, dumbfounded.

Finally, Shimon the Canaanite, said harshly

- "I will not let us be killed! If they try, I will fight back!"

Gently I said to him

- "You will not be killed, not at this time. I will have to leave you, and you will have to hide. I will teach my final lesson here on Earth by myself, for as yet, only I can give this sign."

- "But master", Petros said pleadingly, "you can teach many years to come, you can make thousand more into believers. Our work has just begun!"

- "You are right, Shimon", I said, "your work has just begun. But mine is soon finished, at least here and now. What good would it be to gain the whole world, yet forfeit my soul? What can anyone give me in exchange for my soul?"

The twelve stared at the ground, gloomy, at loss for what to say.

Finally, Thaddeus asked

- "When and where will this happen, master? I trust you have seen this in a vision."

- "Yes, brother Yehudah bar Alphaeus", I said, "I have seen this in a vision. And this vision does not end with my death. It continues, and I will live for real. As I have told you, I have come so you may have life, and have it to the full.

But to answer your question: it will happen in Jerusalem, and it will happen next Passover.

And more than this I will not reveal, as each of you will come to many more coming crossroads, where you will have to make your own decisions. But this is where my path will lead me, and I want to follow it, and I have found peace in this. But I ask you to keep this to yourselves, at this point this for your ears only."

None of the Twelve had anything more to say, and our meeting ended by one after one quietly leaving. And I knew that they would probably assemble by themselves, to talk about what I had revealed.

Chapter 19. Quintilus 21 786.
Transfiguration.

The next day, I, Shimon Petros, Hakob the Elder and Ohannes went away by ourselves. I had asked them to accompany me up into the area of Mount Hermon, to meditate.

They were still taken with what I had told them the day before, and we walked together in silence a couple of hours.

In the far distance we could see the snowy peaks of the mountain, but we were heading to a nearby crest which was high, but where it was still warm at this time of the year. On the way up we found a mountain creek with cold water, and we filled our water sacks, and drank our fill of the cool, fresh water.

When we reached the summit after three hours of rather strenuous climbing uphill, we sat down on the sheep skins we had carried with us, and ate bread and dried fish and drank of the water. It felt like having the whole world at your feet; we could see far into Syrian Phoencia to the west, far into Trachonitis to the south, and the snowy peaks of Mount Hermon to the north and east.

- "I know", I said, "that what you heard yesterday, about my vision of my path, disturbs you. I have asked you to follow me here today to meditate, and to open your hearts to the voice of Allah."

- "I am disturbed, as you say", Shimon Petros said, "but more than that: I grieve and I am scared. This should not be."

- "After today you will still feel sorrow, but you will not harbor fear", I said, "but let us not talk, let us open up, to be as open as this sky."

Sitting facing each other in a circle, we closed our eyes, and went into meditation. As there was no wind, and we had left both birds and insects behind us on our way up to this altitude, it was completely quiet. My mind became as quiet, and as open as the sky, and there were no thoughts, no emotions. I just felt the presence of the mountain below and the vast sky above.

After what could have been a long time, as I had no sense of time, I sensed light, it was as if the sun had come out from behind clouds. I opened my eyes, and I saw it was not the sun. The light came from me, and was reflected in the others, and by the white sheep skins we sat on. It looked as if I had caught fire with flames white of intense heat, but there was no heat, just the light.

The other three had opened their eyes as well, and sat paralyzed, looking at me, their eyes round, mouths open. Slowly, I stood up. Words came, and I said

- "In this moment, Moses is on his mountain, and Allah speaks to him."

And to my left I could see Moses, clad in white, white light shining from within him. And I said

- "In this moment, Elijah is on his mountain, and Allah speaks to him."

And to my right stood the old but tall figure of Elijah, white light shining from within. Despite the clear sky, thunder was heard, and despite the still air, the roar of a storm could be heard, and despite stillness, the violent movement of and earthquake could be felt. I looked up into the sky and said

- "And in this moment, I am on my mountain, and Allah speaks to us, to all of us."

The images of Moses and Elijah faded away, and inside my skull I could hear a booming voice that said

- "You are my beloved son. Listen to more than your thoughts and your words and you will always know that I am present."

And it became completely quiet again, and the white light faded slowly.

When I turned my eyes down again I could see Petros, Hakob and Ohannes lying down on the ground, as if they were sleeping.

I sat down, and I touched them gently. After a while they awoke slowly and sat up, one after the other. We sat looking at each other, for a long time, in silence.

Finally, Petros said

- "I do not know when I fell asleep. The high mountain air must have made me do so. But, it feels like I have had a lucid dream. A dream I will remember all my life, this dream will never fade."

- "Shimon Petros, my brother", I said, "I ask you now, for you to know whether this was a dream or not: tell us exactly of what happened."

And Petros slowly told us, including all details. Hakob and Ohannes looked at him, more and more astonished, and when Petros had finished his description, Ohannes said

- "This was no dream. I have shared your vision, this happened to me as well, just as you described it!"

Hakob said

- "No, this was neither dream nor vision. It happened. But it felt like Allah spoke to me, even when He directed His words to you, master Yeshua."

I said

- "Allah spoke to the three of us. What He said is true for each one of us. It is true for any man, but He wants us to hear this clearly today, as we have a Mission of His to fulfil."

- "But why", Ohannes asked, "did I sleep? Why did you have to wake us up? Have we not just shared the same dream?"

- "You did not sleep when it happened", I said, "but fell asleep when it stopped. This is your earthly mind's way of protecting itself to the light, which would dispel your earthly mind completely if you had stayed awake."

- "So if I would have stayed awake, I would have died?" Hakob asked.

- "No, you would have come alive to your True Self", I said, "but your time has not yet come."

- "I know now that this has happened, I know that Allah just spoke to me, but my earthly mind, as you call it", Petros complained, "does not comprehend this. What does He mean saying that his voice is neither words, thoughts or emotions?"

- "This", I said slowly, "is an important question, Petros. Words, thoughts and emotions are of your earthly mind. Sounds of thunder, the roaring of a storm, the earth shaking, and other signs like this, are also of the earthly mind. The voice of Allah is something entirely different, and it needs not be heard as a sound, it needs not be interpreted, when we truly listen to it, we know.

To know is to have awoken completely. You are not there yet, and most of your time you are left having words, thoughts and emotions. But if they are used for Allah, they can *point* at Truth, even if they in themselves *are* not Truth itself.

But today you have heard, and from today you *know*. But this knowledge is something you cannot put words on."

- "Yes, now I know", said Ohannes, "but I do not know how I know. I just know. It is as you said before, Yeshua, fear is gone, even if I feel sorrow for what you say will happen in Jerusalem."

- "One last thing I want to ask you, before we start ascending this mountain to return to our camp", I said. "I ask you to explain to the other nine of the Twelve, with words that will come to you as you speak, why they need not fear."

- "If I tried to do it now, I would not know how to do it", Hakob said, "but when you say 'with words that will come as I speak' I trust they will, and I will do what you ask. Thank you, master Yeshua, for bringing us here today."

We stood up, embraced each other, long, warm embraces, each one of us with each one of the others.

We packed our things, and wandered back again. Sometimes we talked about the plans for the days and weeks ahead, but during long periods of time we walked in silence, in our own thoughts.

Chapter 20. Ianuarius 10 787.
El'azar.

We had travelled south again. There was unrest in Samaria, so I had sent out seventy of my followers ahead to seek out friendly villages in Judea where we could stop.

After three months traveling southwards with many gatherings with people wanting to hear our message, where many found themselves and were healed, we reached Jerusalem and participated in the Feast of Tabernacles.

We lived a while in Miryam Magdalene's old home in Bethany, together with her sister Marta and her brother El'azar, friends as well as believers since long.

After this we returned to our camp outside Jerusalem, to participate in Hanukkah, the Feast of Lights, where I had some harsh confrontations with the priests, after which we decided to leave Jerusalem for Perea.

The day before this day, Ianuarius 10, we got message from Miryam that her brother El'azar had taken seriously ill, and I and the Twelve went there as quickly as we could. At the time we were in Bethabara in Perea, east of Jordan, and we arrived here in Bethany in the afternoon.

When we entered the house, we saw El'azar in his bed, which they had carried out into the front room.

Many of their friends and neighbors stood around in small groups, talking quietly, many cried.

Miryam rushed up to me, crying, and said

- "You are too late, Yeshua, he died at noon!"

I hugged Miryam, and I said

- "It is never too late to awaken, Miryam."

- "We are not talking about spiritual things now, Yeshua, my brother is dead!" Miryam angrily retorted, tears swelling in her eyes, "we have already anointed him and we are waiting for the rabbi to arrive."

- "I am not mocking you, dearest Miryam", I said, tears coming in my eyes as well, seeing my dear brother El'azar lying there before me, "and I want us all to take each other by the hands and I will pray for him. His soul lives."

Astonished by my words, everyone gathered around the bed. We were almost thirty people. Near El'azar's head, I and the Twelve placed ourselves, together with El'azar's sisters Miryam and Marta, and we all took each other's hands. I said

- "El'azar, my dear friend. For my inner eye I see you, well and alive. I see you alive with your ideas, your strong emotions, and your passion."

Miryam seemed to understand what I was doing, and she continued

- "El'azar, my dearest brother. I see you for my inner eye. How you love to discuss with me and our sister. I see your love and your devotion."

And Marta caught on, and said

- "El'azar, dearest brother. I see you for my inner eye. I see your warmth, your compassion for the weak and suffering. I see you so full of energy, wanting to do so much."

And each one in the ring, one after the other, talked warmly, from their hearts, to El'azar. Each one remembered one more fine thing about him, each one acknowledged him for who he was.

Finally, when everyone had spoken, I said

- "El'azar, wake up, your time has not yet come! You have much left to accomplish. Rise!"

Everyone looked at me, with expressions of shock and dismay, some even looked angry, mouths open, ready to say their meaning. But from El'azar came a deep sigh, and all eyes returned to him.

And El'azar's eyes slowly opened, and his chest rose as he breathed in deeply. Everybody gasped, a few sank to the floor, their faces pallid by shock. It was completely silent.

Supporting himself with his elbows, El'azar sat halfway up, and looked around. First he looked astonished, then embarrassed, and he said

- "I must have fainted. I had a fever and I was dizzy, and then at once it got dark and I froze, as if the night had suddenly returned. But why are you all standing here? What has happened?"

- "El'azar, my brother", I said and took him by his shoulders, "rise from you bed and help us prepare food and drink, because we are all here to celebrate your healing, and to celebrate that we together have found our true selves."

- "You rose my brother from death!" Miryam cried, and grabbed my arm. "You really are the Messiah, the Son of Allah!"

At her words, many cried out, some knelt and touched the floor with their foreheads. I held my hand up, and after a while everybody became silent again, looking at me.

- "Yes, Miryam, my sister", I said gently, "I am the Son of Allah, but I am not a Messiah, I am the Awakener. And you are a Daughter of Allah, and we here are all Sons and Daughters of Allah. Together we have seen El'azar's true Self, together we have believed he is a Son of Allah eternally, and as we have believed, so have we seen."

El'azar rose from his bed. He staggered, because he was still faint, but with the support from his sisters he soon stood erect, breathing deeply, and he said

- "I feel well! I have not felt as well for a long time! Yes, Yeshua, let us put food and wine on the table! Miryam, Marta, go to the market and buy a lamb and more wine."

- "We will all together prepare the feast", I said and smiled at him, "but first, I want you all to join me in giving thanks to our Lord, for inviting us to this feast."

And together, we prayed, and the ones who had not heard these words before, listened to them and remembered them:

> "Our Father who art in heaven.
> Hallowed be thy Name.
> Thy Kingdom is here.
> Thy will be done, on earth as in heaven.
> Give us what we truly need and
> forgive us our mistaken thoughts,
> for us to forgive others for theirs.
> Help us see temptation,
> so that we avoid doing evil.
> Ours is the Kingdom, and the power,
> and the glory, for ever and ever.
> Amen."

Chapter 21. Aprilis 12 787.
The Last Supper.

We were back in the house of Miryam, Marta and El'azar, the Twelve and I. We had traveled from Judea in order to be here for the Passover week, and we had been going into Jerusalem every day.

We had got word during our last stay here that Caiaphas and the Sanhedrin had before Pontius Pilatus accused me of blasphemy and for instigating rebellion during my preaching in the Temple. Because of this we had left Jerusalem once again, this time putting our camp up north in Ephraim, Judea, from there making tours around Perea during two months.

As usual, we had gathered many people, we had preached and taught and many awakened. In one village, two blind persons had found themselves and regained their vision, and people suffering from leprosy had cleansed their minds of sick beliefs and had also healed themselves, but foremost, many had healed their minds and had found peace within themselves. Again, the people healed as well as witnesses of the healing attributed this to my magic powers, but I had given up in trying to make them believe otherwise. Persistently, though, I reminded each one that their changed beliefs and their faith was what had healed them.

Despite the insistent warnings from my disciples, I had decided that we would return to Jerusalem for

Passover, to continue to preach in the Temple. Many of the Twelve seemed to still believe in the coming of the New Kingdom on Earth, and this was unfortunately also what they taught the masses. But I let them be, as I knew that the coming of New Inner Kingdom, the Awakening, would take root only if many seeds were planted, and this had to be done at the heart of peoples' mistaken belief in the Demanding Allah: in the Temple.

We arrived on Palm Sunday, and I had instructed some of the disciples to borrow a donkey that I would ride, to signify that I did not come as a king, but as an ordinary man. Despite this, people welcomed us already at the entrance to the town, spreading palm leaves on my path, and singing.

When my disciples saw me crying when I rode through the entrance, they thought I was moved by the peoples' hails, but I did not tell them that my tears came from remembering my vision from my childhood of the total destruction of the town and of the Temple. I now knew that this was going to happen only a few decades into the future.

We returned to the Temple on Monday, Tuesday and Wednesday, each evening returning to Bethany. For each day of preaching at the Temple, the Sadducees had become more and more questioning, and pressed me for explanations of the message we were giving about the coming Kingdom of Heaven. I felt blessed that the Sadducees and the Pharisees partook with such fervor in the Plan - their persistent questioning and accusations helped us sow so many more seeds in peoples' minds and hearts.

Today Thursday we had decided to rest, and I and the Twelve were lying on rugs in the front room of Marta's and El'azar's house, after the midday meal.

- "Miryam, there is much left to put away!" Marta said impatiently through the door out to the inner court. "Don't just sit there, come here and help me!"

- "Marta, dear sister", I said and smiled at her, "that can surely wait, sit down with us. Learn patience. Miryam is sitting here at my feet, as are my other disciples. We have much to discuss."

Marta snorted with disapproval, and disappeared from the door.

- "But you should not go in to Jerusalem today", Shimon said, "it is too dangerous. We others can be there, and we can preach ourselves. It is you the Sanhedrin see as a prophet threatening their power and threatening Rome, not us."

- "My Mission is not finished, and my Path is laid down", I said, "and when I enter Jerusalem tonight, it will be the start of the New Kingdom in the hearts of those who want to listen. My Mission is to use myself as the Message, the Message that will live, after my body has died."

- "But I do not understand", said Shimon, "why shall we eat dinner in the town tonight? What is it that will happen tomorrow so early that we cannot go from here?"

- "I have asked you to rent the big room", I said, "so that we can eat by ourselves, just you the Twelve and I, because I have an important message for you, a message that you shall spread around the world in the time to come."

- "If you are leaving our house tonight", Miryam said, tears in her eyes, "let me prepare your feet for tomorrow."

And she left the room, and returned with a bottle of precious oil, richly flagrant with flower essence. She sat down again at my feet and anointed them thoroughly. Seeing this, Yehudah Iscariot said

- "Woman, why do you use that oil for anointing feet, we could have sold it and gotten many shekels for the needy tomorrow!"

- "Yehudah", I said, "let her do what she needs to do, as she will not be able to do this at my burial. To give is to receive. To receive all, give all."

- "But the Kingdom is near", he objected angrily, "and you will not die before it comes. All the prophesies say so!"

- "My dear brother Yehudah", I said, "when I am dead, people will discover that the Kingdom has already been here all the time. It has been here since Adam and Eve fled from the Garden of Eden. Everyone who is willing to listen will be able to open their eyes and they will be saved. But be on your way now, and do what you need to do."

The others assumed I was sending him on some errand in preparation for our supper coming evening, but when I saw him leave, a tense look on his face, I knew that his fear was driving him, and I felt sad. From Nicodemus I had heard that Yehudah had discussed the establishing of a new Judean authority in the New Kingdom to come, with some of the younger Pharisees. His stubborn belief in the Messiah was blinding him, and I knew that his good intentions would turn against him.

***

We sat all of us, Shimon Petros, Andreas, Philippos, Nethanel, the two Hakobs, Ohannes, Matthias, Thaddeus, Yehudah Te'oma, Shimon the Zealot, Yehudah Iscariot, and I, around the big supper table in the upper room of the house Shimon Petros had rented.

Before they entered the room, I had insisted on cleaning their feet with a bucket of warm water and a linen cloth, and they were still embarrassed by this.

- "I understand you did this, master", said Hakob the younger, "to signify that you do not regard yourself as different from us. But really, washing the feet of others is for women and for slaves!"

- "We are all sons and daughters of Allah, and truly I tell you", I said, "in the new Kingdom to come no one will be a slave to another, and women will have the same rights as men. Allah who sees us truly does not put different values on us, he never judges. To Him we are all the same, Children of Allah, created in His likeness."

- "I find that hard to believe, it goes against all common sense. But explain again, master", Thaddeus pleaded, "how the new Kingdom will come. I cannot understand why you will have to die. Not even Shimon Petros, Hakob the Elder and Ohannes who shared the vision with you on Mount Hermon can explain this."

- "I know you are saddened that I will die tomorrow", I said, "and I am myself terrified at the pain I know I will experience. But you should also rejoice, as I do, because my death will not be an ending. From my death the New Kingdom will arise. But it will not be a kingdom of the world, it will be a kingdom from inside yourself, an experience you will awaken to. After my death I will send the Holy Spirit down into your minds and hearts, and you will awaken, and you will go out into the world and awaken others."

- "Will there be a new rule then?" Yehudah Iscariot asked.

- "No, my brother Yehudah", I said and sighed a little, "there will be no change of how the Earth is ruled, not for a long time. There will be in the far future, but that new rule will be the result of an inner awakening, where people more and more will be able to see each other as Sons and Daughters of Allah. When this starts to happen, and you twelve will be the first to have this ability, the world will more and more become a happy dream, instead of the sad dream it is now."

- "You have spoken much of reaching this happy dream", Matthias said, "but explain once again, how is it that forgiveness leads there?"

- "Because", I said slowly, "the world we experience today, the dream of sorrow, of lack and of death, is something we think exists because we think we have sinned against our Father. Without knowing it with our thoughts, we believe deep down that evil, suffering and sickness is the punishment from Allah for our sins and that we have to make sacrifices at the Temple to atone for this. But we are mistaken. We are mistaken! There is no punishment, there has never been, and we have made up the suffering against ourselves. We have ourselves made up death. There – Is – No - Death."

- "Forgiveness", I continued, after having let them absorb what I just said, "is not forgiveness of sins.

When I say to people 'Your sins are forgiven', I really mean 'I forgive you for having mistaken yourself, believing that you have sinned'. This is too difficult for many to understand as yet, but it is crucial that *you* understand this."

- "When I forgive someone completely and fully this way", I said, "I see this person as the perfect, sinless Child of Allah he or she is, and my seeing this makes it possible for them to see it as well. Those who do so heal themselves, and it is this you have witnessed. It is this that *you* will be able to help people with now, and I want you to go out in the world and do what I have done, in my name."

Yehudah put his hands to his face, and his body shook. Everyone looked at him, surprised, but no one said anything. Finally, he lowered his hands, cheeks wet with tears, and said, sobbing

- "What have I done? I have misled myself, and I have misled others. I have brought this upon us. I have even taken money from the money box I have been appointed to manage, to give to the Pharisees cooperating with me. I thought they would help us when the day of the New Kingdom would come, and when we here would rule the twelve tribes of Israel, at your side…"

- "Yes, Yehudah", I said calmly, "you have misled yourself, and I have seen you do this. And also for these mistaken thoughts are you forgiven. You did what you thought was right, but you were mistaken.

You are forgiven not because you now repent; you are forgiven because nothing has happened. Nothing real can be threatened. Nothing unreal exists. Herein lies the peace of Allah."

- "It is I who deserve death for what I have done. And they are going to kill you because of nothing. You are no threat, you are the savior." Yehudah sobbed, but I could sense that he was unable to accept forgiveness, and I felt sad for him, knowing that he would punish himself.

- "But now my brothers", I said, and took a loaf of bread from the basket on the table. "Let use share this bread."

And I broke the bread into pieces and I walked around the table to give each one of my twelve disciples one piece each, and I said

- "When you meet in remembrance of me, share your bread to signify how we as brothers and sisters share with each other all what we need here on Earth."

I took a sack of wine, and I walked around the table and poured everyone wine, and I said

- "When you meet in remembrance of me, share your wine to signify how we as brothers and sisters share with each other what comes from the Holy Spirit in Heaven."

And we all ate, and we drank the wine. Despite the anxiety and tension that we had come with, coming into the town, being very near the Temple and the palace of Caiaphas, the High Priest, a sense of peace now spread. We ate the plentiful food and drank the wine that Shimon Petros and Andreas had arranged, and we spent the evening in more and more relaxed talk, as if the impending doom did not exist.

Near midnight, I broke up and we walked together out through the East Gates, to the tranquil Garden of Gethsemane on the Mount of Olives, for an evening prayer by ourselves, as we had planned before.

Chapter 22. Aprilis 13 787.
The crucifixion.

We had come to the Garden of Gethsemane. I went up on Mount of Olives by myself to pray. The peacefulness from the supper had now gone, and I felt sadness of what would happen, both to me and to all others. The large group of people that had followed me for more than three years would now scatter, and many would be killed in my name. The Twelve would survive the turmoil, but many of them would eventually also become killed because of me, although far in the future.

I knew well that my Path was laid out, and that there was no return, but even so, I felt suddenly weak, and I prayed, trembling with fear:

- "Father, you gave me once a Chalice, with which I would save the world. If you are willing, take this cup from me. But be not my will, but thine, Father."

And suddenly the Angel from my childhood stood there before me. He was not as big as I remembered Him, and I realized that I now was as tall as He. The white light that shone from within Him was strong, but not as blinding as then. It was mild and gentle, and I could feel how the light entered my mind and my soul, and how it filled me with peace.

He smiled gently at me and said

- "Yeshua, my child, you have drunk from this chalice, and you have become a strong man, the leader of men and women. Drink now the last bitter drop, and you will give others the sweet Wine of Life that they will never thirst again."

And He faded slowly, and I stood alone in the darkness again.

I went down into the garden again, and saw with the light from my oil lantern that all of the Twelve had laid down on the ground, exhausted by their anxiety and sorrow. I put my lantern down on the ground and pulled each one up by his hand, and I embraced each one, long embraces without words.

Yehudah hurried up to me and said

- "Master. Because of my talking with the priests, they surely know that we will come here, so we must leave at once!"

- "I know, Yehudah", I said, "but it is too late. They are already at the gate. My Path is laid and will not change."

In his anguish, Yehudah clung sobbing to me, as a drowning man trying to save himself.

At this we heard twigs cracking under heavy boots, we saw many lanterns, and a troop of many soldiers came through the trees into the clearing we occupied.

The commander looked around, got sight of Yehudah, who he obviously recognized, and asked, pointing at me:

- "Is this the one claiming to be the king of the Jews, the one planning to bring down the Temple?"

Shimon Petrus stepped in front of us and drew the short sword he always carried against bandits on the roads.

- "I am the one you are looking for", I said, gently pushing Shimon to the side. "Shimon, put down your sword. Those who use the sword will be killed by sword."

- "You are arrested for instigating rebellion", said the commander, "and you will follow us. The rest of you are not charged with anything as for now, and you can leave."

***

In complete darkness, I sat against the cold and damp stone wall of a dungeon outside the West Wall of the Temple, down into which the soldiers had thrown me. I could hear moanings from others nearby, but I could not see how many there were. My arms were aching, as the soldiers had tied them behind my back with a rope around my wrists.

After many hours, the weak light of dawn that found its way through the hole in the roof of the dungeon made it possible to see, and I saw two others, which also sat leaning with their backs against a wall. One of them was badly beaten, blood covered his face.

- "You arrived to our fine lodging tonight", one of the men said, "what brings us the honor?"

- "I am Yeshua bar Yosef from Nazareth", I said, "who are you, and why have they imprisoned you?"

- "I am Ari bar Benaiah from Amasa, and my bloody friend is Obed bar Nadab from Etam. Our crime is that we stood listening to the zealots outside the Temple."

- "What are you accused for?" I asked.

- "They just called us bandits. But every time a zealot gets caught, they call them that. So I suppose they think we belong to that group. We don't, but they will not listen."

- "No, they see only what they believe", I said.

- "But, are you Yeshua the Nazarene, are you not the one they call the king of the Jews?" Ari asked. "Could your followers not protect you?"

- "Had they tried they would have been here with us", I said, "and they will do their work without me now."

Now Obed cleared his throat and said

- "Are they really going to tear the Temple down? Is that what will happen now? I have heard you have thousands of followers."

- "The Temple is but a symbol for temples of belief people have built in their minds. In three days I will tear these temples down and I will build new ones."

- "I have heard that you have the thoughts of a madman", Obed muttered, "and now I hear you do. These words will not save you from the cross."

At this we heard noise from above, and a wooden ladder came down through the round hole in the roof. Two soldiers came climbing down, and they beckoned me to rise. One tied a rope round my chest, and a guard in the room above hoisted me up, the soldiers pushing me from underneath.

The soldiers then ordered me to follow them, and the guard walked behind me, holding the rope to prevent me from running away. Behind us they led Ari and Obed, also secured with ropes. We walked the empty roads up north. The sun had just risen from behind the buildings, and there were but a few people around to be seen. The ones that saw us just glanced, and then continued with what they were doing – prisoners led by guards were surely a common sight in these quarters.

We arrived at Fort Antonia just north of the Temple, and the soldiers pushed me impatiently up the stairs - from their comments I understood that they were anxious to be back soon for their morning meal which had been delayed by the task to bring me here.

I was led into a large room, where I recognized the prefect Pontius Pilatus. He sat at a large desk, studying some scrolls, and he did not look up when I entered with the soldiers.

- "This is him, your Excellency", one of the soldiers said, standing at attention in front of the desk, "the man from Nazareth, the agitator at the Temple."

Pilatus turned his head up and looked at me, and asked

- "Which of the agitators? The one Caiaphas said had threatened to tear down the Temple? Are you the one they call the king of the Jews, the one they say will throw us Romans out?"

- "My kingdom is of another kind, and it is open for everyone", I said.

- "If you Jews could just abide by your laws and follow your traditions, I would not need to spend so much time with all these wild-heads", Pilatus muttered, scribbled his signature on a piece of papyrus, and handed it to the soldier standing at his desk. "Take care of this one and the other two at once."

And with this, he turned back to his work at the desk.

The soldiers led me out again, this time into the inner court of the fort.

***

Ari and Obed had been brought to the inner court as well. The former soldiers had been replaced by new ones, and these had removed our clothes, leaving us with only our loin cloths. They laid heavy wooden planks over our shoulders and tied them to our wrists. It was getting hot, and we were all three sweating.

One of the soldiers had made jokes about "the king of the Jews", and had made a crown of thistles, which he pushed down around my head. The thorns had cut my forehead, and I had to blink my eyes all the time to see through the trickles of blood coming down my face.

They pushed us in front of them out through the entrance of the fort. The street outside was full of onlookers, there to watch the spectacle of today. My thirst was beginning to make me feel dizzy and I stumbled and fell. Two of the soldiers grabbed the plank, and violently pulled me up, and one pushed his spear against my back to get me to continue towards the west gate. Another one gave me a heavy lash with his whip over my back.

Coming through the gate, the execution mound Golgotha could be seen. The crosses from days before still carried corpses, where the dogs during the night had chewed the meat of the legs and the feet, and where crows and scavenger vultures still now and then hacked the faces.

When we reached the top of the mound, the soldiers forced us down on the ground, and with sledges they drove nails through our wrists. I fainted at the pain, but awoke again when they hoisted us up on three wooden poles, that I saw had been prepared for us, as the one I was hung up on had a crude wooden sign above me saying "King of the Jews". I could not see to read the text string, but I heard one of the soldiers cry it out mockingly, pointing at the sign.

The soldiers then held my legs against the pole, one leg at each side, and they drove large iron nails through my heels. This time I did not faint, so I was immediately able to breathe again by standing on the nails through the feet, thus releasing the strain in my arms from hanging.

When the soldiers were ready, they sat down on the ground around us, to guard against anyone trying to take a victim down. Most of the spectators had now left, but outside the circle of soldiers there remained a few, and I could hear women crying.

Obed, who was hanging left of me, shrieked

- "If you are the Son of Allah, why don't you save us?"

But Ari, on my right side, said with a low voice

- "Yeshua, when you come to your kingdom, think of me."

- "Ari and Obed, my brothers", I said hoarsely, "forgive these soldiers, and you will be in my kingdom before me. Forgive them, for they do not know what they do. You will not die, only your bodies will."

I could see that Obed, weak because of his beating the day before, could not any longer stand, and he sagged down more and more. The strain in his arms made it soon impossible for him to breathe, and his head fell down as he fainted. I could hear him draw his breath a couple of times more, the last breaths minutes between, and then he died.

Ari and I became weaker and weaker as well, and we could talk no more, having to use all our strength to keep standing on the nails through our heels. We stood for many hours. I lost sense of time, but the sun passed its highest point and its heat felt like fire.

The sweat had now washed away the blood in my eyes, and I could see the people beyond the soldiers clearer, and I suddenly recognized Miryam from Magdala and a couple of the other women in our group. They were standing embracing each other, all crying bitterly.

I cried out at her, the pain in my arms and in my legs almost unbearable. She came as close as she could before one of the soldiers stood up and stopped her by holding his spear against her.

- "Master Yeshua!" she cried, wringing her hands.

- "Miryam", I said, but then my voice failed me, as my throat was completely dry.

The soldier holding the spear, went to his group, took a piece of cloth, wetted it from a leather pouch. He came up to me, and reached up on his toes and pressed the cloth into my mouth. I pressed my yaws together, and could take one gulp of the sour wine in the cloth. The soldier took it out again, and went back to stop Miryam from coming closer.

- "Miryam ... my sister ...", I said with the last of my dwindling strength,

"It ... Is ... *Not* ... Finished. ... Believe ... And ... You ... Will ... See."

And the strength went from my legs that had been trembling more and more violently from the strain of trying to remain standing, and I sagged down. I could feel an excruciating pain in my chest, as the pull from my arms stopped me from breathing, and it went black.

Chapter 23. Aprilis 16 787.
Resurrection.

I had been outside of time, and I knew that my old friend Nicodemus, together with his friend, Yosef of Arimathea, a member of the Sanhedrin, had persuaded Pilatus to let them bury me, instead of just letting my body remain on the cross, as they usually did.

I stood inside the tomb Yosef had arranged. It was dark in the tomb chamber as the entrance stone had been rolled before the opening, but I willed light, and I could see my body lying on the tomb shelf, wrapped in linen cloth, a scent of myrrh and aloe spreading from it.

I let my old body, my tool for being in the world to fulfil Allah's Mission, cease to be, and the cloth sank down, flat on the stone shelf.

I knew that now when the Sabbath was over, Miryam and the other women would come here to clean the body from blood, and I waited outside. There sat two soldiers on guard - Pontius, even if he had agreed to let Yosef take the body from the cross contrary to the custom, had been afraid my followers would steal the body.

Miryam and three other women from our group arrived, and they got the soldiers to open the grave. The stone was heavy, and both of the soldiers had to push hard to move it aside. Miryam went into the tomb, but returned out at once:

- "He is gone!" she cried. "Only the wrapping is left! Quickly, get Shimon Petrus and the others here! I will wait so that no one touches anything."

The other women did not first obey, as they wanted first to see for themselves, but soon they ran away. The soldiers, confused, also went in, Miryam following. They all came out, and the soldiers rushed away as well.

I made myself visible to Miryam, and when she saw me she cried angrily

- "Grave guard! Where have you put him? Show me at once, so that we can care for him!"

- "Miryam, my sister", I said. "Believe and you will see."

Miryam stared at me, looking utterly confused, then terrified.

- "It is I", I said, "be not afraid. Remember I said to you: it is *not* finished."

She sank down on her knees, trembling, and said

- "Master Yeshua. I know. But how…"

- "You do not need to understand", I said gently, and sat down on the grass beside her, "you just need to know that I am here."

I took her by her hands. She continued to tremble, as with high fever, but eventually she calmed herself, and sunk down from her kneeling to sit on the grass as I did, and we sat looking at each other. Finally, a happy smile spread on her face, and she said

- "I do not understand. My head cannot take this in. But in my heart I know you are really back. My hands feel your warmth. Are you real? Or are you a ghost, am I seeing things in my confusion?"

- "If you by real mean if this is my earthly body", I said, "no, it is not. But I am more real than I have ever been. I am no ghost, this is not a vision. I am I."

I took her in my arms and I hugged her. She started to cry, as if awakening from a nightmare where one is at the same time still in shock from the terror of the dream and crying in relief that it was only a dream. After long time, her crying abated, and she sighed and asked

- "What will happen now?"

- "I want you to stay here, I will leave now. When Petros, Ohannes, and the others come, tell them what has happened here, and tell them that I will meet them three days from today, in the room where we had our last supper."

Chapter 24. Aprilis 19 787.
The New Beginning.

I was at the upper room in the house just south of Caiaphas palace, just inside the door, which I knew was firmly locked from the inside. All of the Twelve were there, except Yehudah Iscariot, who in his misery and inability to accept my forgiveness had killed himself.

They sat around the large table, and they just had eaten.

Yehudah Te'oma, sitting with his back to the door, said

- "Women's' stories! The court does not approve of a testimony from a woman or from a slave, as we all know they do not have the same strength of the mind as we men. Why then should we believe differently?"

- "Because, brother Yehudah", I said, "the only difference between a woman's mind and ours is their greater ability to observe things keenly."

Yehudah, and the other ones sitting on his side of the table turned quickly around. Everyone stared, mouths open, paralyzed.

- "Miryam thought first I was a ghost, but I trust she told you that she found me to be real", I said smiling, and walked up to them.

I took Yehudah by the shoulders, rose him up, and hugged him warmly. He was first tense like a wooden scarecrow, but then he relaxed, and tears flowed down his cheeks, wetting his beard, and he said

- "Yeshua, my dearest brother. What my eyes cannot believe, my body and my nose does. It *is* your familiar embrace, it *is* your scent. It *is* really you."

He took a step back from me, smiling, but then he looked confused again and said

- "But where are the wounds? Miryam and the women told us about the crown of thistles cutting your forehead and about the iron nails through your wrists!"

- "Yehudah, as I have said before", I smiled, "I love your keen mind. You are right, this is me, but I have let my old body cease to be. It was my faithful servant and my obedient tool for being on Earth, to fulfil my Mission, and it has fulfilled its purpose. I am showing myself to you in a physical body identical to your memories, so that I may be with you like this for one last time today. But I assure you, ghosts are illusions of a misguided mind, and I am no illusion. I am really here with you. I will be with you from this day on, but from the days to follow, I will not be appearing like this. I will speak to your souls and minds directly, in the form of the Holy Spirit. Sometimes you will hear my voice, sometimes you will just get my thoughts."

And I went to each one of them, and we embraced each other, and I said:

- "Andreas bar Jonas. You were my first disciple, and you brought others to me. I love your optimism and your humbleness. You shall travel north, to preach my word, to heal with your hands, and to awaken people in my name."

- "Shimon Petrus bar Jonas. You were my second disciple, and you have been the rock foundation of this group. Your passion will make people believe. You will go to Rome, to build my church there.

- "Philippos of Beth-Saida. You were the third to follow me. You have a warm heart but a pessimistic head. Which is good, because you will need to be alert when you go to Greece and to Scythia in the north-east, were I am sending you to spread the message about me in the tongue of your father, and to heal people.

- "Nethanel bar Talmai. You who wondered whether anything good could come from Nazareth. What do you think now? You will fulfil your mission in Arsacid Armenia in the east, teaching all that there is no death.

- "Hakob bar Zebedee. Your mother tried to persuade me to give you fine positions in my kingdom. You I will ask to stay here in Jerusalem, to continue to spread the message here. This is your fine position, and you will awaken many."

- "Ohannes bar Zebedee. Your mission is to spread my word in the northwest. They are sometimes slow to learn, and a son of thunder like you is well fitted to awaken them."

- "Matthias bar Alphaeus. You will with your keen mind and warm heart teach the Normans in Dacia, up north-west. Perform miracles in my name!"

- "Hakob bar Alphaeus, Hakob the Just. You are needed here in Jerusalem as well, to preach to the Jews and to awaken them and to help my brother Hakob. When you are ready here, I want you to go to Hispania, to turn them into believers."

- "Thaddeus bar Alphaeus. You who have combined both zeal and tenderness in your heart. I want you to go to Babylon, where you will meet many talking our tongue."

- "Yehudah Te'oma. With your Essene skepticism and your wisdom you shall bring my word far east to the Satavahana Empire. On your way there you might well meet people who remember me from thirteen years ago. You will find the instructions you need for your travel in Qumran."

- "Shimon the Canaanite. I am sending you to Egypt, and when you have awoken people there, you shall continue westward, to the Briton and Saxon provinces of the Roman Empire."

After this, we all sat down, and for many hours I answered many questions that they all had, and we talked about what had happened after they saw me be led away by the soldiers until today, and about their missions I had instructed them to take on.

I saw that Yehudah still looked skeptically at me, so I asked him

- "I am hungry. Do you have any food left?"

He looked surprised, but then he looked embarrassed and he smiled when he saw me eat the bread and fish he gave me, and he smiled even broader seeing me wash it down with wine.

Ohannes said

- "We are now eleven messengers. Will there be more apostles?"

I said

- "Anyone spreading my message according to what I have taught is my apostle. In the near future I will call a few more myself, and they will do great deeds. But over the eons to come, many will be called in many different ways, not many will listen, but some will. My message will come through in new ways, in different languages, in many different forms all together.

But you who have been with me these three years, you have listened. I called you to follow me, and you left everything behind and you followed. I trust you to continue to spread the Truth, and to spread the message about that which I now have proved beyond any doubt - there is no death. The Happy Truth that there is no hell and no sin. These are things we have invented to keep ourselves imprisoned.

When we forgive each other, and when we forgive ourselves these mistaken thoughts, we can awaken to The Happy Dream, which is Allah's Kingdom on Earth. And when everyone has awoken, we will all go home to heaven, to return to the Oneness with our Father, who has never left us."

- "But, master Yeshua", Yehudah Te'oma said, "already we eleven sometimes have different ways of understanding what you have said, not to speak of the hundreds of your followers in our larger group. How shall we be able to remain truthful to what you really mean?"

- "This is a very important objection, thank you for bringing this up Yehudah", I said. "There will be many teachings in my name that will spread a message different from mine. There will even be scriptures about me called holy that will spread messages that completely contradict what I am saying. Your most bitter enemies will not be the pagans, it will be the ones who claim that *their* version of my message is the Truth."

- "So how are we, and how are our followers going to be able to know what is what?" Ohannes asked.

- "There is one way, a way that always will work", I said. "You remember how I have taught you that there is no sin, there is no pure evil. There are only two things that make people act. One of these is fear, the other one is love. Fearsome people act in destructive ways, that hurt others but foremost they hurt themselves, by becoming more and more imprisoned in their own mistaken beliefs.

From what the tree gives, you will know if the tree is healthy: if the fruit is good, nourishes you and gives you peace, then it is the tree of Truth. If the fruit tastes bitter and makes you anxious and fearful, then it has grown on a sick tree.

Whatever problem you encounter, whatever pain people suffer, whatever people do to you, there is only *one* response that works in the long run, and that is unconditional Love."

- "So, to answer your question, Ohannes", I continued. "If a message engenders love and leads to people forgiving each other, then this message is probably true. If a message engenders fear, and leads to persecution, judgment and demands for repentance and sacrifice, then this message is most probably false."

Shimon Petrus sighed, and said

- "Master. Your teaching sounds so simple, but it will be the most difficult thing mankind ever has tried to learn. The old way of thinking has been for so long. But if what you are asking us to do works, if the sowing of these seeds of new fruit trees leads to seeds taking root and new trees to grow, then this is really a new beginning."

- "Yes, Shimon, my Rock", I said, "this *is* The New Beginning."

www.ingramcontent.com/pod-product-compliance
Lightning Source LLC
Chambersburg PA
CBHW071203160426
43196CB00011B/2177